THE COMPLETE BOOK

Hors-d'Oeuv

DAVID J RODGERS

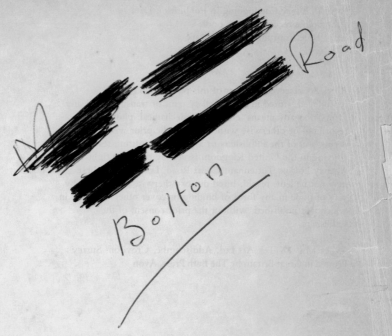

Pitman

PITMAN PUBLISHING
128 Long Acre, London WC2E 9AN

A Division of Longman Group UK Limited

© David Rodgers 1992

First published in Great Britain 1992

British Library Cataloguing in Publication Data
A catalogue record for this book
is available from the British Library

ISBN 0273 03779 X

Typeset by ⅍ Tek Art Ltd, Addiscombe, Croydon, Surrey
Printed in Great Britain by The Bath Press, Avon

*To my father, who encouraged me
in my career and passed away before
this project was completed.*

Contents

Introduction

The main purpose of this recipe book is to help the catering student produce a variety of hors-d'oeuvres and larder preparations to a high standard. The preparations covered are put together by the Larder Chef or *Garde Manager* who can be counted among the most skilled of chefs. She or he has to have a great deal of knowledge about commodities, what to do with them and how to put them together to produce a dish containing taste, colour, texture and atrractiveness.

This book is designed to help improve skills in an area of food preparation that is sometimes forgotten as the first thing the customer sees when they go out to eat. First impressions really do count. Cold buffets, single and compound hors-d'oeuvres and salads, savoury snacks and other tasty morsels are the gastronomic introduction to a fine meal.

The Complete Book of Hors-d'oeuvres encourages the reader to use their imagination and experiment. The text is easy-to-use, so not exclusive to the catering student but relevant to all people with an interest in cookery, be it as a hobby or on a professional basis. The variety of commodities used in cookery has increased as growing, preserving and exporting techniques have improved. The demand for exotic vegetables has increased, and many people use new and wonderful ingredients to enhance and improve their meals, in the home and in restaurants. Gone are the days when one could not get anything but round lettuce, for example. Now in every supermarket there are at least five varieties in stock, from cos to lollo rosso.

Choice is the key today. More people are weaning themselves off high fat content foods and varying their diets to much more healthy alternatives. With this publication you can extend your repertoire and your knowledge of dishes and their make-up.

Enjoy the preparation and cooking of these recipes and the happiness you give to the people for whom you cook.

1
BASIC RECIPES

Court Bouillon

FISH COOKING LIQUOR

Yield: 1l (2 pints)

Quantity		Ingredients	Preparation
1l	2 pints	water	
10g	½oz	sea salt	
50g	2oz	carrots	sliced
	1	bay leaf	
10g	½oz	parsley stalks	
60ml	⅛ pint	vinegar	
	10	black peppercorns	
50g	2oz	onions	sliced
	1 sprig	thyme	

Method

1 Simmer all the ingredients together for 30 minutes before use.

Épice de Charcutiére

LARDER SEASONING

Yield: 275g (9oz)

Quantity		Ingredients
50g	2oz	thyme
50g	2oz	bay leaves
25g	1oz	cloves
10g	½oz	mace
35g	1½oz	black peppercorns
25g	1oz	allspice
15g	¾oz	nutmeg
10g	½oz	ginger
10g	½oz	marjoram

Method

1 Pound all the ingredients together in a mortar until they are very finely ground.
2 Pass through a fine sieve to remove any remaining lumps.

To store

Store in a plastic bag in a jar.

Uses

Seasoning.

Gelée Ordinaire

ASPIC JELLY

Yield: 4½l (1 gallon)

Quantity		Ingredients	Preparation
400g	1lb	chicken giblets	
400g	1lb	minced chicken	
250ml	½ pint	egg whites	
	2½	lemons	juiced
4½l	1 gallon	white stock	strained and cooled
400g	1lb	leaves gelatine	soaked in cold water

Method

1 Mix the giblets, chicken, egg whites and lemon juice together.
2 Add the stock.
3 Drain the gelatine, then add it to the stock.
4 Heat the mixture until it reaches boiling point, stirring.
5 A 'crust' will form, but do not remove it or stir it back in.
6 COOK OUT for aproximately 2 hours.
7 Strain through muslin.
8 Leave the resulting liquid to cool and set.

Service

Use as required, melting it just before use.

Uses

As required.

Variations

Replace chicken giblets and minced chicken with 800g (2lb) minced whiting or sole for Fish Aspic. Replace 250ml (½ pint) of the white stock with that quantity of madeira, for Madeira Aspic.

Le Sel d'Épice

SPICED SALT

Yield: 150g (6oz)

Quantity		Ingredients
100g	4oz	table salt
20g	1oz	white pepper
20g	1oz	Les Épice Fine (see page 6)

Method

1 Carefully weigh all the ingredients.
2 Mix well together.

To store

Store in a plastic bag in a jar.

Uses

Seasoning.

Variation

Mix together the same amount of salt with 50g (2oz) each of allspice, paprika and mace and 25g (1oz) of nutmeg for a different Sel d'Épice.

Les Épice Fine

FINE SPICES

Yield: 150g (6oz)

Quantity	Ingredients
70g 3oz	white pepper
30g 1oz	paprika
10g ½oz	mace
5g ¼oz	nutmeg
5g ¼oz	cloves
5g ¼oz	marjoram
5g ¼oz	rosemary
5g ¼oz	cinnamon
5g ¼oz	bay leaves
5g ¼oz	sage

Method

1 Weigh all the ingredients carefully.
2 Pound in a mortar until very finely ground.
3 Pass through a fine sieve to remove any remaining lumps.

To store

Store in a plastic bag inside a jar.

Uses

Seasoning.

Panada

BREADCRUMB, FLOUR OR RICE MIXTURE

Yield: 250g (½lb)

Quantity		Ingredients
250ml	½ pint	milk
50g	2oz	butter
	pinch	nutmeg
		salt and pepper
125g	5oz	flour *or* breadcrumbs *or* rice

Method

1 Bring the milk, butter and seasonings gently to the boil.
2 Remove the pan from the heat, add the flour or breadcrumbs or rice, stir until the mixture is smooth, then return the pan to the heat to COOK OUT over a gentle heat for about 3–4 minutes, when it should be cooked and have thickened.
3 Spoon the mixture onto a buttered tray, smooth it out and leave to cool before using.

Uses

Panada is a stiff mixture that is added to fish, meat, poultry and game forcemeats to help bind the mixtures together or to extend them.

2
SAUCES AND DRESSINGS

Chiffonade Dressing

Coulis de Fraise

Coulis de Framboise et Fraise

English Mustard Dressing

Fines Herbes Dressing

French Mustard Dressing

Lemon Dressing

Marseillaise Dressing

Mayonnaise

Mayonnaise Colée

Paprika Dressing

Roquefort Dressing

Saint Regis Dressing

Sauce Aïoli

Sauce Andalouse

Sauce Citron

Sauce Cumberland

Sauce Oxford

Sauce Gribiche

Sauce Marie Rose

Sauce Menthe

Sauce Niçoise

Sauce Raifort

Sauce Ravigote

Sauce Remoulade

Sauce Tartare

Sauce Verte

Stilton Dressing

Terrine Covent Garden Sauce

Thousand Island Dressing

Tomato Dressing

Vinaigrette

Chiffonade Dressing

EGG AND BEETROOT VINAIGRETTE

Yield: 500ml (1 pint)

Quantity		Ingredients	Preparation
375ml	¾ pint	oil (olive *or* groundnut)	
125ml	¼ pint	vinegar, distilled	
	2	eggs	hard boiled, sieved
10g	½oz	beetroot	cooked and cut into BRUNOISE
	¼tsp	parsley	finely chopped
		salt and pepper	

Method

1 Measure the oil and vinegar into a bowl.
2 Mix well together.
3 Add the sieved egg, beetroot and parsley and mix well.
4 Season to taste.

Uses

As required.

Service

Sauce-boat, DISH PAPER, FLAT.

Coulis de Fraise

STRAWBERRY SAUCE

Yield: 500ml (1 pint)

Quantity		Ingredients	Preparation
800g	2lb	frozen strawberries	
	2	lemons	juiced
50g	2oz	castor sugar	

Method

1 Liquidise the strawberries until smooth.
2 Pass through a *CHINOIS* to remove any remaining lumps.
3 Season to taste with the lemon juice and sugar.

Uses

As required.

Service

As required.

Coulis de Framboise et Fraise

STRAWBERRY AND RASPBERRY SAUCE

Yield: 500ml (1 pint)

Quantity		Ingredients	Preparation
200g	8oz	frozen strawberries	puréed
200g	8oz	frozen raspberries	puréed
200ml	8fl oz	water	
	½	lemon	juiced
50g	2oz	castor sugar	
5g	¼oz	arrowroot	

Method

1 Place the fruit purées, water and lemon juice in a pan.
2 Bring to the boil, then add the sugar.
3 Dilute the arrowroot with a teaspoonful of cold water, pour the mixture into the boiling sauce, stirring and COOK OUT.
4 Pass through a CHINOIS to remove any lumps and pips.
5 Leave to cool.

Service

Adjust the consistency, if required, with a little stock syrup.

Uses

As required; delicious with fruit hors-d'oeuvres.

English Mustard Dressing

Yield: 500ml (1 pint)

Quantity	Ingredients
375ml ¾ pint	oil (olive or groundnut)
125ml ¼ pint	vinegar, distilled
	salt and pepper
¼tsp	English mustard powder

Method

1 Measure the oil and vinegar into a bowl.
2 Season to taste and mix well together.
3 Add the mustard to taste and mix it in well.

Uses

As required.

Service

Sauce-boat, DISH PAPER, FLAT.

Fines Herbes Dressing

HERB VINAIGRETTE

Yield: 500ml (1 pint)

Quantity		Ingredients	Preparation
375ml	¾ pint	oil (olive or groundnut)	
125ml	¼ pint	vinegar, distilled	
	1tsp	parsley	finely chopped
	1tsp	chives	finely chopped
	1tsp	tarragon	finely chopped
	1tsp	chervil	finely chopped
		salt and pepper	

Method

1 Measure the oil and vinegar into a bowl.
2 Mix well together.
3 Add the herbs and season to taste.

Uses

As required.

Service

Sauce-boat, DISH PAPER, FLAT.

French Mustard Dressing

Yield: 500ml (1 pint)

Quantity		Ingredients
375ml	¾ pint	oil (olive or groundnut)
125ml	¼ pint	vinegar, distilled
	½tsp	French mustard
		salt and pepper

Method

1 Measure the oil and vinegar into a bowl.
2 Mix well together.
3 Add the French mustard, season to taste and mix well.

Uses

As required.

Service

Sauce-boat, DISH PAPER, FLAT.

Lemon Dressing

Yield: 500ml (1 pint)

Quantity	Ingredients
375ml ¾ pint	oil (olive or groundnut)
125ml ¼ pint	lemon juice
	salt and pepper

Method

1 Measure the oil and lemon juice into a bowl.
2 Season to taste and mix well together.

Service

Sauce-boat, DISH PAPER, FLAT.

Uses

As required.

Marseillaise Dressing

GARLIC VINAIGRETTE

Yield: 500ml (1 pint)

Quantity	Ingredients	Preparation
375ml ¾ pint	oil (olive or groundnut)	
125ml ¼ pint	vinegar, distilled	
½ clove	garlic	crushed
	salt and pepper	

Method

1 Measure the oil and vinegar into a bowl.
2 Mix well together.
3 Add the crushed garlic and season to taste.

Uses

As required.

Service

Sauce-boat, DISH PAPER, FLAT.

Mayonnaise

Yield: 500ml (1 pint)

Quantity		Ingredients
4		egg yolks
	¼tsp	English mustard powder
500ml	1 pint	groundnut oil
	1tsp	vinegar
		salt and pepper

Method

1 Place the egg yolks and mustard in a mixing bowl.
2 Gradually whisk in the oil.
3 When the sauce becomes thick, add the vinegar and season to taste.

Uses

As required.

Service

Thin to correct consistency with vinegar if necessary.

Mayonnaise Colée

SET MAYONNAISE

Yield: 500ml (1 pint)

Quantity		Ingredients	Preparation
	4	egg yolks	
	¼tsp	English mustard powder	
500ml	1 pint	groundnut oil	
	1tsp	vinegar	
25g	1oz	gelatine	soaked in cold water
		salt and pepper	

Method

1 Place the egg yolks and mustard in a mixing bowl.
2 Gradually whisk in the oil.
3 When the sauce becomes thick, add the vinegar.
4 Melt the soaked gelatine in a tablespoonful of hot water or lemon juice and add it to the basic mayonnaise.
5 Season to taste prior to use.

Uses

As required, but especially where binding or coating of ingredients is required.

Paprika Dressing
PAPRIKA VINAIGRETTE

Yield: 500ml (1 pint)

Quantity		Ingredients	Preparation
375ml	¾ pint	oil (olive or groundnut)	
125ml	¼ pint	vinegar, distilled	
50g	2oz	onions	finely chopped
	1tsp	paprika	
		salt and pepper	

Method

1 Measure the oil and vinegar into a bowl.
2 Mix well together.
3 Add the onions to the dressing and mix them in.
4 Season to taste with the paprika and salt and pepper.

Service

Sauce-boat, DISH PAPER, FLAT.

Uses

As required.

Roquefort Dressing

ROQUEFORT VINAIGRETTE

Yield: 500ml (1 pint)

Quantity		Ingredients	Preparation
375ml	¾ pint	oil (olive or groundnut)	
125ml	¼ pint	vinegar, distilled	
		salt and pepper	
50g	1oz	Roquefort cheese	finely grated

Method

1 Measure the oil and vinegar into a bowl.
2 Season to taste and mix well together.
3 Add the cheese and mix it in.

Service

Sauce-boat, DISH PAPER, FLAT.

Uses

As required.

Saint Regis Dressing

MUSTARD AND WORCESTERSHIRE SAUCE VINAIGRETTE

Yield: 500ml (1 pint)

Quantity	Ingredients
375ml ¾ pint	oil (olive or groundnut)
125ml ¼ pint	vinegar, distilled
	salt and pepper
¼tsp	English mustard powder
¼tsp	Worcestershire sauce

Method

1 Measure the oil and vinegar into a bowl.
2 Season to taste and mix well together.
3 Add the mustard and Worcestershire sauce to the dressing to taste.

Uses

As required.

Service

Sauce-boat, DISH PAPER, FLAT.

Sauce Aïoli

GARLIC MAYONNAISE

Yield: 500ml (1 pint)

Quantity		Ingredients	Preparation
	4	egg yolks	
	¼tsp	English mustard powder	
500ml	1 pint	groundnut oil	
	1tsp	vinegar	
	¼oz	garlic	finely chopped
		salt and pepper	

Method

1 Place the egg yolks and mustard in a mixing bowl.
2 Gradually whisk in the oil.
3 When the sauce becomes thick, add the vinegar.
4 Add the garlic to the mayonnaise.
5 Correct seasoning and consistency, if necessary, for the intended use. (If a thinner consistency is required, use a teaspoonful of boiling water per 500ml/pint of sauce.)
6 Season prior to use.

Service

Sauce-boat, DISH PAPER, FLAT.

Uses

As required.

Sauce Andalouse

PINK SPICY MAYONNAISE

Yield: 500ml (1 pint)

Quantity		Ingredients	Preparation
	4	egg yolks	
	¼tsp	English mustard powder	
500ml	1 pint	groundnut oil	
	1tsp	vinegar	
100g	4ozs	tomato ketchup	
	¼tsp	Worcestershire sauce	
	¼tsp	Tabasco sauce	
25g	1oz	sweet red pimento	cut into julienne
		salt and pepper	

Method

1 Place the egg yolks and mustard in a mixing bowl.
2 Gradually whisk in the oil.
3 When the sauce becomes thick, add the vinegar.
4 Add the tomato ketchup to produce a pink sauce.
5 Add Worcestershire and Tabasco sauce to taste.
6 Mix in the julienne of pimento.
7 Season prior to use.

Service

Sauce-boat, DISH PAPER, FLAT.

Uses

As required.

Sauce Citron

TOMATO, HERB AND LEMON SAUCE

Yield: 20 portions

Quantity		Ingredients	Preparation
400g	1lb	tomatoes	make into a CONCASSER
5g	¼oz	tarragon	finely chopped
5g	¼oz	parsley	finely chopped
25g	1oz	tomato ketchup	
	1	lemon	juice
750ml	1½ pint	plain yogurt *or* fromage blanc	

Method

1 Place all the ingredients in a bowl and whisk them together well.

Service

To accompany the Hure de Saumon aux Poivre Vert avec Sauce Citron (see page 180).

Uses

Evening menu.

Variations

Derivatives

Sauce Cumberland

REDCURRANT AND PORT WINE SAUCE

Yield: 250ml (½ pint)

Quantity		Ingredients	Preparation
200g	8oz	redcurrant jelly	
125ml	¼ pint	port wine	
25g	1oz	shallots	finely chopped
	1	lemon	
	1	orange	
	1tsp	English mustard powder	
	¼tsp	cayenne pepper	
	¼tsp	ground ginger	

Method

1 Melt the redcurrant jelly with the port wine.
2 Blanch and refresh the shallots.
3 Cut the orange and lemon zest into fine julienne, then blanch and refresh.
4 Squeeze the juice out of the lemon and orange and dissolve the mustard in it.
5 Add the juice, zest and shallots to the redcurrant and port sauce.
6 Leave to cool.
7 Add the cayenne pepper and ginger just before serving and, if necessary, adjust consistency for intended use. (For a thinner consistency, add a teaspoonful of boiling water per 500ml/pint of sauce.)

Service

As required.

Uses

As required, but ideal with cold, cooked meats.

Variation

As above but cut the zest into fine dice for Sauce Oxford.

Sauce Gribiche

MAYONNAISE WITH GHERKINS, CAPERS, HERBS, ANCHOVY AND EGG

Yield: 500ml (1 pint)

Quantity		Ingredients	Preparation
	4	egg yolks	
	¼tsp	English mustard powder	
500ml	1 pint	groundnut oil	
	1tsp	vinegar	
100g	4oz	gherkins	finely chopped
50g	2oz	capers	finely chopped
25g	1oz	parsley	finely chopped
25g	1oz	onions	finely chopped
10g	½oz	tarragon	finely chopped
10g	½oz	chives	finely chopped
10g	½oz	anchovy fillets	finely chopped
	2	eggs	hard-boiled
		salt and pepper	

Method

1 Place the egg yolks and mustard in a mixing bowl.
2 Gradually whisk in the oil.
3 When the sauce becomes thick, add the vinegar.
4 Mix the gherkins, capers, parsley, onions, tarragon, chives and anchovy fillets with the mayonnaise.
5 Separate the hard-boiled egg into white and yolk, finely chop the yolk and cut the white into a julienne.
6 Mix the prepared egg carefully with the other ingredients.
7 Season prior to use.

Service

Sauce-boat, DISH PAPER, FLAT.

Uses

As required, but delicious with fried and grilled fish.

Sauce Marie Rose

PRAWN COCKTAIL SAUCE

Yield: 500ml (1 pint)

Quantity		Ingredients
	4	egg yolks
	¼tsp	English mustard powder
500ml	1 pint	groundnut oil
	1tsp	vinegar
100g	4oz	tomato ketchup
	¼tsp	Worcestershire sauce
	¼tsp	Tabasco sauce
		salt and pepper

Method

1 Place the egg yolks and mustard in a mixing bowl.
2 Gradually whisk in the oil.
3 When the sauce becomes thick, add the vinegar.
4 Add the tomato ketchup to produce a pink sauce.
5 Season to taste with the Worcestershire and Tabasco sauce.
6 Season prior to use.

Service

Sauce-boat, DISH PAPER, FLAT.

Uses

As required, but very good with fish and shellfish cocktails.

Sauce Menthe

MINT SAUCE

Yield: 250ml (½ pint)

Quantity		Ingredients	Preparation
100g	4oz	mint leaves	washed and dried
50g	2oz	sugar	
	2tbsp	water	
125ml	5fl oz	vinegar, distilled	
		salt and pepper	

Method

1 Finely chop the mint leaves.
2 Add the chopped mint to the other ingredients.
3 Correct seasoning and consistency, if required.

Service

Sauce-boat, DISH PAPER and FLAT.

Uses

Roast lamb dishes.

Sauce Niçoise

NIÇOISE VINAIGRETTE

Yield: 500ml (1 pint)

Quantity		Ingredients	Preparation
375ml	¾ pint	oil (olive *or* groundnut)	
125ml	¼ pint	vinegar, distilled	
	1tsp	French mustard	
25g	1oz	capers	finely chopped
25g	1oz	stuffed olives	finely chopped
25g	1oz	parsley	finely chopped
25g	1oz	anchovy fillets	finely chopped
		salt and pepper	

Method

1 Measure the oil and vinegar into a bowl.
2 Mix well together.
3 Add the French mustard to taste.
4 Add the capers, stuffed olives, parsley and diced anchovy and season to taste.

Service

Sauce-boat, DISH PAPER, FLAT.

Uses

As required, but especially good with cold meats and egg dishes.

Sauce Raifort

HORSERADISH SAUCE

Yield: 250ml (½ pint)

Quantity		Ingredients	Preparation
125ml	5fl oz	double cream	
75g	3oz	fresh horseradish	grated
		salt	
		cayenne pepper	

Method

1 Whip the cream until it forms soft peaks.
2 Fold in the grated horseradish.
3 Season to taste with the salt and cayenne pepper, correct the consistency, if necessary, with a little water (the sauce should have the consistency of lightly whipped cream).

Service

Sauce-boat, DISH PAPER and FLAT.

Uses

Serve with roast beef and smoked fish.

Sauce Ravigote

HERB, SHALLOT AND CAPER VINAIGRETTE

Yield: 500ml (1 pint)

Quantity		Ingredients	Preparation
375ml	¾ pint	oil (olive or groundnut)	
125ml	¼ pint	vinegar, distilled	
		salt and pepper	
25g	1oz	shallots	finely chopped
5g	¼oz	parsley	finely chopped
5g	¼oz	tarragon	finely chopped
5g	¼oz	chervil	finely chopped
10g	½oz	capers	finely chopped

Method

1 Measure the oil and vinegar into a bowl.
2 Season and mix them together well.
3 Add the rest of the ingredients and mix together.

Service

Sauce-boat, DISH PAPER, FLAT.

Uses

As required.

Sauce Rémoulade

MUSTARD, HERB, CAPER AND ANCHOVY MAYONNAISE

Yield: 500ml (1 pint)

Quantity		Ingredients	Preparation
	4	egg yolks	
	¼tsp	English mustard powder	
500ml	1 pint	groundnut oil	
	1tsp	vinegar	
100g	4oz	gherkins	finely chopped
50g	2oz	capers	finely chopped
25g	1oz	parsley	finely chopped
25g	1oz	onions	finely chopped
10g	½oz	tarragon	finely chopped
10g	½oz	chives	finely chopped
10g	½oz	anchovy fillets	finely chopped
		salt and pepper	

Method

1 Place the egg yolks and mustard in a mixing bowl.
2 Gradually whisk in the oil.
3 When the sauce becomes thick, add the vinegar.
4 Mix the remaining ingredients into the mayonnaise.
5 Season prior to use.

Service

Sauce-boat, DISH PAPER, FLAT.

Uses

As required, but delicious with fried and grilled fish.

Sauce Tartare
TARTARE SAUCE

Yield: 500ml (1 pint)

Quantity		Ingredients	Preparation
	4	egg yolks	
	¼tsp	English mustard powder	
500ml	1 pint	groundnut oil	
	1tsp	vinegar	
100g	4oz	gherkins	finely chopped
50g	2oz	capers	finely chopped
25g	1oz	parsley	finely chopped
25g	1oz	onions	finely chopped
		salt and pepper	

Method

1 Place the egg yolks and mustard in a mixing bowl.
2 Gradually whisk in the oil.
3 When the sauce becomes thick, add the vinegar.
4 Mix the remaining ingredients into the mayonnaise.
5 Season prior to use.

Service

Sauce-boat, DISH PAPER, FLAT.

Uses

As required, but very good with fried fish.

Sauce Verte

GREEN MAYONNAISE

Yield: 500ml (1 pint)

Quantity		Ingredients	Preparation
	4	egg yolks	
	¼tsp	English mustard powder	
500ml	1 pint	groundnut oil	
	1tsp	vinegar	
75g	3oz	spinach	cooked, refreshed, then patted dry
5g	¼oz	tarragon	chopped
5g	¼oz	chervil	chopped
5g	¼oz	chives	chopped
5g	¼oz	watercress	chopped
		salt and pepper	

Method

1 Place the egg yolks and mustard in a mixing bowl.
2 Gradually whisk in the oil.
3 When the sauce becomes thick, add the vinegar.
4 Place the spinach, tarragon, chervil, chives, watercress and a little oil in a food processor or blender and blend until fine.
5 Mix them well with the mayonnaise until it turns an even green colour.
6 Correct the seasoning and consistency, if necessary, for the intended use. (If a thinner consistency is required, use a teaspoonful of boiling water per 500ml/pint of sauce.)
7 Season prior to use.

Service

Sauce-boat, DISH PAPER, FLAT.

Uses

As required, but especially good with poached salmon.

Stilton Dressing

STILTON VINAIGRETTE

Yield: 500ml (1 pint)

Quantity		Ingredients	Preparation
375ml	¾ pint	oil (olive or groundnut)	
125ml	¼ pint	vinegar, distilled	
		salt and pepper	
50g	2oz	Stilton cheese	finely grated

Method

1 Measure the oil and vinegar into a bowl.
2 Season to taste and mix well together.
3 Add the Stilton to the dressing and mix it in well.

Service

Sauce-boat, DISH PAPER, FLAT.

Uses

As required.

Terrine Covent Garden Sauce

VEGETABLE TERRINE SAUCE

Yield: 125ml (5fl oz)

Quantity		Ingredients
500ml	1 pint	chicken stock
100g	4oz	tomato purée
100g	4oz	tomatoes
500ml	1 pint	red wine vinegar
500ml	1 pint	olive oil
		salt and pepper
250ml	½ pint	double cream

Method

1 Blend the first four ingredients together in a food processor or blender.
2 Add the olive oil slowly, then season.
3 Just before serving, mix in the cream.

Service

Serve with the Terrine Covent Garden (see pages 267–8).

Uses

Variations

To make a thicker sauce, replace the cream with 2 egg yolks.

Derivatives

Thousand Island Dressing

Yield: 500ml (1 pint)

Quantity		Ingredients	Preparation
375ml	¾ pint	oil (olive or groundnut)	
125ml	¼ pint	vinegar, distilled	
25g	1oz	shallots	finely chopped
5g	¼oz	parsley	finely chopped
5g	¼oz	tarragon	finely chopped
5g	¼oz	chervil	finely chopped
10g	½oz	capers	finely chopped
	¼	cucumber	peel, finely dice
	2	eggs	hard-boiled, finely chopped
	1 clove	garlic	finely chopped
10g	½oz	gherkins	finely chopped
	½	red pepper	finely chopped
	½	green pepper	finely chopped
25g	1oz	tomato	made into a CONCASSER
		salt and pepper	

Method

1 Put all the ingredients except the salt and pepper into a bowl.
2 Mix them well together.
3 Season to taste.

Uses

As required.

Service

Sauce-boat, DISH PAPER, FLAT.

Tomato Dressing

Yield: 500ml (1 pint)

Quantity	Ingredients	Preparation
375ml ¾ pint	oil (olive or groundnut)	
125ml ¼ pint	vinegar, distilled	
	salt and pepper	
100g 4oz	tomatoes	made into a CONCASSER

Method

1 Measure the oil and vinegar into a bowl.
2 Season to taste and mix well together.
3 Add the CONCASSER, adjust the seasoning, if necessary, and mix well.

Service

Sauce-boat, DISH PAPER, FLAT.

Uses

As required.

Vinaigrette

Yield: 500ml (1 pint)

Quantity	Ingredients
375ml ¾ pint	oil (olive or groundnut)
125ml ¼ pint	vinegar, distilled
	salt and pepper

Method

1 Measure the oil and vinegar into a bowl.
2 Season to taste and mix together well.

Uses

As required.

Service

Sauce-boat, DISH PAPER, FLAT.

3
COLD SOUPS

Crème d'Avocat Parisienne

AVOCADO SOUP

Portions: 4

Quantity	Ingredients	Preparation
2	avocados, ripe	
125ml ¼ pint	white wine	
1	lemon	juiced
	salt and pepper	
1 bunch	mint	take the leaves off the stems, discard the stems and wash the leaves
250ml ½ pint	single cream	
125ml ¼ pint	natural yogurt	
125ml ¼ pint	milk	
Garnish		
1	avocado, ripe	sliced

Method

1 Cut the 2 avocados in half and remove the stones.
2 Skin and roughly chop the flesh.
3 Liquidise the avocado with the wine and lemon juice.
4 Season and add the mint leaves.
5 Pour into a mixing bowl.
6 Add the cream and yogurt.
7 Adjust the seasoning and thin to desired consistency with the milk, if necessary.

Service

Serve in a tureen or consommé cups, garnished with the avocado slices.

Uses

Buffets as an hors-d'oeuvre.

Crème Caroline

COLD CREAM OF SWEETCORN SOUP

Portions: 4

Quantity		Ingredients	Preparation
25g	1oz	onion	finely chopped
35g	1½oz	butter	
275g	11oz	tinned sweetcorn	drained and washed
875ml	34 fl oz	milk	
	pinch	nutmeg	
		salt	
Garnish			
	pinch	paprika	
	1tbsp	chives	finely chopped

Method

1 Sweat the onion in the butter.
2 Add the sweetcorn to the onion and cook for 2 minutes.
3 Pour in the milk, season with the nutmeg and salt and bring to the boil.
4 Simmer for 5 minutes.
5 Purée in a blender, then pour through a CHINOIS.
6 Chill until cold.

Service

Serve in a tureen or individual soup bowls, garnished with the paprika and chives.

Uses

Variations

Derivatives

Crème Vichyssoise
LEEK AND POTATO SOUP

Portions: 4

Quantity		Ingredients	Preparation
50g	2oz	butter	
200g	8oz	white of leek	trimmed, washed and chopped
150g	6oz	onions	finely chopped
400g	1lb	potatoes	peeled, washed and chopped
1 litre	2 pints	white chicken stock	
750ml	1½ pints	milk	
		salt and pepper	
Garnish			
250ml	½ pint	cream	
10g	½oz	chives	finely chopped

Method

1 Melt the butter and sweat the leek and onions in it.
2 Add the potatoes.
3 Add the stock, milk and seasoning.
4 Simmer for 1 hour.
5 Liquidise, pass through a sieve, return to the pan and bring back to the boil.
6 Adjust the seasoning and consistency, if necessary, to light coating consistency with a little water.
7 Leave to go cold.

Service

Serve the soup in a tureen. Garnish with a swirl of the cream and the chives.

Uses

An hors-d'oeuvre.

Crème Vichyssoise aux Courgettes

COLD CREAM OF COURGETTE SOUP

Portions: 4

Quantity		Ingredients	Preparation
800g	2lb	courgettes	
200g	8oz	potato	
	2tsp	salt	
1½l	3½ pints	water	
		salt and pepper	
150ml	7fl oz	double cream	lightly whipped
Garnish			
10g	½oz	parsley	chopped
10g	½oz	chives	chopped
10g	½oz	chervil	chopped

Method

1 Peel the courgettes, cut them in half lengthways, scoop out the seeds and roughly cut into 5cm (2-inch) pieces.
2 Peel the potato and cut into 1.5cm (½-inch) dice.
3 Salt the water and bring to boil. Add the courgettes and potatoes and boil for 13 minutes once the water returns to boil.
4 Drain the vegetables and save the liquid. Leave them to cool.
5 Purée the vegetables and 200ml (8fl oz) of the cooking liquor in a liquidiser.
6 Season with pepper and blend until smooth.
7 Leave to cool for 10 minutes then fold in the lightly whipped cream.
8 Chill for 2 hours.

Service

Serve in a soup tureen or in soup bowl and garnish with the chopped herbs.

Soupe de Concombre Lebanese

LEBANESE CUCUMBER SOUP

Portions: 4

Quantity		Ingredients	Preparation
400g	1lb	cucumber	washed
	2 cloves	garlic	peeled
	1tbsp	tarragon vinegar	
	½ bunch	mint	pick the leaves from the stem, throw away the stems and wash the leaves
		salt and pepper	
250ml	½ pint	single cream	
125ml	¼ pint	natural yogurt	
Garnish			
10g	½oz	gherkins	finely chopped
25g	1oz	peeled prawns	finely chopped
	8	mint leaves	washed

Method

1 Chop the cucumber into small pieces.
2 Liquidise the cucumber with the garlic, tarragon vinegar, mint and seasoning.
3 Pour into a mixing bowl and blend with the cream and yogurt.
4 Pass the soup through a CHINOIS.
5 Adjust seasoning and consistency, if necessary, to a light coating consistency with water.

Service

Place the gherkin and prawns in the bottom of a tureen or consommé cup, then add the soup. Arrange the mint leaves on top.

Uses

Buffets and as hors-d'oeuvre.

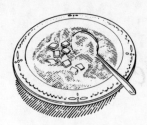

Dialogue de Purée aux Fruits

SELECTION OF FRUIT PURÉES

Portions: 4

Quantity		Ingredients	Preparation
175g	7oz	apricots	blanched, skinned and stoned
120ml	4fl oz	mineral water	
350g	14oz	mangoes	peeled and stoned
175g	7oz	strawberries	cleaned
	½	lemon juice	
		castor sugar	
175g	7oz	blackcurrants	cleaned and de-stemmed
225g	9oz	apples	peeled and cored
175g	7oz	raspberries	
		apple juice	
Garnish			
		mint leaves	
		kiwi fruit	
		strawberries	

Method

1 Purée the apricots in a blender, strain and thin down with a little of the mineral water, if it is very thick and dry, then chill.
2 Purée the mango flesh, strain and thin down with the mineral water, if it is very thick and dry, then chill.
3 Purée the strawberries, strain and add a little of the lemon juice and sugar, depending on the sweetness or tartness of the strawberries, then chill.
4 Bring the blackcurrants to the boil in 2 tablespoons of water with a little lemon juice and sugar, depending on the sweetness or tartness of the blackcurrants. Leave to cool, then purée, strain, thin down with a little of the mineral water, if it is very thick and dry, then chill.

5 Cook the apples until they are very soft in a minimum amount of water with a little lemon juice and sugar, depending on the sweetness or tartness of the apples. Leave to cool, strain, thin down with a little apple juice, if it is very thick, then chill.

6 Purée the raspberries, strain and add a little lemon juice and sugar, depending on the sweetness or tartness of the raspberries, thin down with mineral water, if it is very thick, then chill.

Service

Place a scoop of each purée on a chilled plate, with the darkest one in the middle and the other colours carefully arranged around it. Knock the plate firmly to ensure that the purées run together. Garnish with the mint leaves and kiwi fruit and strawberreis.

Variations

Use any suitable other fresh fruits when available.

_____

_____

_____

Derivatives

_____

_____

_____

Gazpacho Andalouse

COLD VEGETABLE SOUP

Portions: 4

Quantity		Ingredients	Preparation
50g	2oz	breadcrumbs	sieved
	1tbsp	tarragon vinegar	
	1tbsp	olive oil	
300g	12oz	tomatoes	blanched and skinned
	2 cloves	garlic	peeled
200ml	8fl oz	tomato juice	
100g	4oz	red pimento	cored, de-seeded
100g	4oz	Spanish onion	peeled
100g	4oz	cucumber	diced
		salt and pepper	
200ml	8fl oz	iced water *or* white wine	
Accompaniments			
100g	4oz	cucumber	peel and cut BRUNOISE
	1	red pimento	cut BRUNOISE
	1	green pepper	cut BRUNOISE
100g	4oz	tomatoes	made into a CONCASSER
25g	1oz	black olives	stoned
50g	2oz	onions	finely chopped
50g	2oz	bread croûtons	toasted

Method

1 Soak the breadcrumbs in the vinegar and oil for 10-15 minutes.

2 Liquidise the breadcrumb mixture together with the remaining ingredients, except the salt and pepper and iced water or white wine.

3 Pass the mixture through a CHINOIS and season.

4 Finish with the iced water or white wine.

Service

Serve the soup in a tureen or consommé cups and the accompaniments on an hors-d'oeuvres tray.

Uses

Buffets and as hors-d'oeuvre.

4
MIXED HORS-D'OEUVRES

Anchovy Dip

Artichaut Vinaigrette

Assiette de Saucisson Assortis/
    Assiette de Charcutière

Assiette de Viande en Gelée

Assiette Poire d'Avocat et Orange

Barquette du Fromage

Boeuf Provençale (1)

Boeuf Provençale (2)

Champignons à la Cru

Cornets de Jambon Astor

Cornet/Roulade de Jambon Garnis

Darioles de Foie Gras

Fonds d'Artichaut Farcis

Fromage Blanc aux Herbes

Gelée de Cassis à la Russe

Jambon de Parme aux Figues

Jambon Fumé aux Pêches

Legumes à la Grecque

Legumes à la Portugaise

Mortadella

Mousse Appareil

Mousse d'Artichaut

Mousse d'Asperge

Mousse de Bouquet

Mousse de Concombre à la Menthe

Mousse de Foie de Volaille

Mousse de Jambon

Mousse de Poivrons Rouges
    Bavarois de Poivrons Trois
    Colors

Mousse de Tomate

Oeufs de Caille Froid au Cresson

Oeufs Durs Froid Moscovite

Oeufs en Gelée

Oeufs Farci

Oeufs Mayonnaise

Oeufs Poche en Gelée Fruits de
    Mer

Oeufs Poches Froid Alexander

Pastrami Salad

Oeufs Poches Froids Frou-frou

Petite Corbeille de Cruditées avec
    Trois Sauces

Poire d'Avocat au Stilton

Poire d'Avocat avec Cresson et
    Sauce Fraises

Poire d'Avocat avec Crevettes

Poire d'Avocat avec Fruits de Mer

Poire d'Avocat Bon Viveur

Poire d'Avocat Epicure

Poire d'Avocat Singapour

Poire d'Avocat Vinaigrette

Poivrons Macerer

Poivrons Provençale

Rillettes de Porc

Rosette Saucisson

Salade de Mange-tout au Gingembre

Salade de Topinambours
   Vinaigrette

Salade de Trois Poivrons et Jambon

Salami de Milan

Sauce Rouille

Tomates à la Monegasque

Tomates Sevigne

Westphalaine Mettwurst

Anchovy Dip

Yield: 5.5l (10 pints)

Quantity	Ingredients	Preparation
2 x 2oz tins	anchovy fillets	
2 cloves	garlic	crushed
1tsp	fresh thyme leaves	
1tsp	fresh ginger	peeled and chopped
1tsp	fresh basil	chopped
2tbsp	Dijon mustard	
2tbsp	lemon juice	
2	eggs	
4tsp	capers	
1tsp	castor sugar	
1tsp	black pepper	
250ml 12fl oz	oil	

Method

1 Put all the ingredients except the oil in a food processor or blender.
2 Process until smooth.
3 Gradually add the oil until the sauce thickens.

Service

Serve in small pots.

Uses

For Petite Corbeille de Cruditées (see page 100).

Variations

_____
_____
_____

Derivatives

_____
_____
_____

Artichaut Vinaigrette

ARTICHOKE VINAIGRETTE

Portions: 4

Quantity		Ingredients	Preparation
	4	artichokes	
	2	lemons	cut 4 slices, squeeze the juice from the rest
5g	¼oz	parsley	washed
250ml	½ pint	vinaigrette	

Method

1 Break off the stalks from the bases of the artichokes.
2 Trim the base flat.
3 Trim the leaves square.
4 Tie a slice of lemon to the base of each of the artichokes.
5 Cook in water to which the lemon juice has been added, covered with a piece of muslin.
6 When tender leave to go cold.
7 Remove the centre (the choke), moving it from side to side to loosen it, then pull it out.
8 Remove the fur from the middle with a teaspoon.
9 Replace the centre, inverted, and put the parsley in the middle.
10 Brush the leaves lightly with the vinaigrette.

Service

Serve the artichokes on a FLAT and serve a sauce-boat of vinaigrette separately.

Uses

Each as single hors-d'oeuvres.

Assiette de Saucisson Assortis

SELECTION OF ASSORTED SAUSAGES

Portions: 4

Quantity		Ingredients	Preparation
25g	1oz	Mortadella	
25g	1oz	Danish salami	
25g	1oz	Bierwurst	
25g	1oz	Cervelat	
25g	1oz	Italian salami	
Garnish			
	2	dill pickles	
	1 bunch	watercress	washed, dried and trimmed

Method

1 Slice the meats thinly, removing skin where applicable.
2 Cut the dill pickles in half and slice thinly almost to the end and fan out.

Service

Arrange the meats on a plate starting with the largest. To make it more interesting, some of the meats may be folded, rolled or made into cornets. Decorate with the watercress and the dill pickle fans.

Uses

Table d'hôte single hors-d'oeuvres.

Assiette de Viande en Gelée

MEATS IN ASPIC

Portions: 4

Quantity		Ingredients	Preparation
500ml	1 pint	aspic (see page 4)	
100g	4oz	ham	sliced
50g	2oz	cooked beef	sliced and cut into julienne
50g	2oz	cooked pork	sliced and cut into julienne
50g	2oz	cooked ox tongue	sliced and cut into julienne
Garnish			
	1	salad of mixed leaves	washed
	1	red pepper	cut into julienne
	1	green pepper	cut into julienne
	1	yellow pepper	cut into julienne
	1	black pepper	cut into julienne
	few slices	garnishing paste	
	1 sprig	fresh dill	

Method

1 Melt the aspic and leave to cool.
2 Line an oval tin mould with half of the aspic and decorate as required.
3 Trim any excess fat off the ham and cut with an oval cutter to fit the prepared mould.
4 Line the inside of the mould with the slices of ham, allowing any excess ham to fold over the top.
5 Fill the mould with the julienned meats.
6 Cover with the excess ham by folding over the meats.

7 Seal the mould with the remaining aspic and leave to set.
8 Dip the mould into hot water for a few seconds to enable the meats to be unmoulded.

Service

Put a plate over the mould and invert, holding the plate firmly to the mould. Tap the mould and lift it off. Decorate with the salad and pepper strips, garnishing paste and dill.

Assiette Poire d'Avocat et Orange

AVOCADO WITH ORANGE AND YOGURT

Portions: 4

Quantity	Ingredients	Preparation
2	avocados	halved and stones removed
4	large oranges	
1	lemon	juiced
125ml ¼ pint	natural yogurt	

Method

1 Peel the avocado halves.
2 Slice thinly but stop just short of one end to form a fan.
3 Rub with the lemon juice to prevent the flesh discolouring.
4 Peel the zest from the oranges and cut it into very fine julienne.
5 Blanch the julienne for 2–3 minutes and run cold water over the strips until they are cold.
6 Carefully peel and segment (see page 128) the oranges.

Service

NAPPER each serving plate with the natural yogurt, coating it evenly. Place an avocado fan in the middle, then garnish with the orange segments and julienned zest.

Uses

Single hors-d'oeuvres.

Barquette du Fromage
CHEESE BOATS

Portions: 4

Quantity		Ingredients	Preparation
100g	4oz	cream cheese	
50ml	2fl oz	cream	
	8	shortcrust pastry barquettes	
	1	lettuce	washed and dried

Method

1 Cream the cheese and cream together.
2 Spoon into a piping bag with a star tube.
3 Pipe decoratively into the barquettes.
4 CHIFFONADE the lettuce.

Service

Place the lettuce over the bottom of a RAVIER dish, place the barquettes on top and decorate as required.

Uses

Hors-d'oeuvres and buffet savouries.

Boeuf Provençale
PROVENÇALE-STYLE BEEF

Portions: 4

Quantity		Ingredients	Preparation
250g	10oz	cooked beef	trimmed and cut into julienne
100g	4oz	tomatoes	made into a CONCASSER
	¼ tin	anchovy fillets	drained and diced
10g	½oz	shallots	finely chopped
5g	¼oz	black olives	stoned
250ml	½ pint	vinaigrette	
	¼tsp	English mustard powder	
	¼tsp	French mustard	
	1 clove	garlic	finely chopped
		salt and pepper	
Garnish			
5g	¼oz	fresh parsley	washed
	a few	salad leaves	

Method

1 Put the beef, tomato CONCASSER, anchovy, shallots and olives into a bowl.
2 Flavour the vinaigrette with the mustards, garlic, salt and pepper.
3 Leave the beef to marinate in the tomato, anchovy, shallots, olives and vinaigrette.

Service

Serve slightly domed on a white SUR LE PLAT DISH or a FLAT with DISH

PAPER and serviette gondala's, garnished with the parsley and salad leaves and serve with a suitable salad.

Uses

Boeuf Provençale

PROVENÇALE-STYLE BEEF WITH POTATOES

Portions: 4

Quantity		Ingredients	Preparation
200g	8oz	potatoes	
250g	10oz	cooked beef	trimmed and cut into julienne
100g	4oz	tomatoes	made into a CONCASSER
100g	4oz	onions	finely chopped
	1 clove	garlic	crushed
250ml	½ pint	vinaigrette	
		salt and pepper	
Garnish:			
	1tsp	chives	finely chopped

Method

1 Cook the potatoes in their jackets, refresh, skin and cut into dice.
2 Put the beef, tomato CONCASSER and onions in a bowl.
3 Mix the garlic with the vinaigrette.
4 Marinate the ingredients in a bowl in the vinaigrette for 20 minutes.
5 Season to taste.

Uses

Service

Serve slightly domed on a white SUR LE PLAT DISH or on a FLAT with DISH PAPER and serviette gondalas with the chives sprinkled over the top.

Champignons à la Cru

MUSHROOMS MARINATED IN MUSTARD AND HERB VINAIGRETTE

Portions: 4

Quantity		Ingredients	Preparation
200g	8oz	small white button *or* wild mushrooms	
250ml	½ pint	vinaigrette	
	1tsp	Dijon mustard	
5g	¼oz	fresh parsley	finely chopped
5g	¼oz	fresh tarragon	finely chopped
5g	¼oz	fresh chervil	finely chopped
Garnish:			
		extra fresh parsley, tarragon and chervil	finely chopped

Method

1 TURN the mushrooms if possible *or* wash and dry them, trim the stalks and then leave whole, half, quarter or slice them, depending on the size of the mushrooms.
2 To the vinaigrette, add the Dijon mustard and herbs and mix together well.
3 Marinate the mushrooms in the vinaigrette for 2 hours.

Service

Serve in a RAVIER dish, NAPPER with the vinaigrette marinade and garnish with the chopped herbs.

Uses

Vegetable hors-d'oeuvres and hors-d'oeuvre varié.

Cornets de Jambon Astor

SET WALDORF SALAD WITH FILLED CORNETS OF HAM

Portions: 4

Quantity		Ingredients	Preparation
500ml	1 pint	aspic (see page 4)	
1 x	recipe	Salade Waldorf (see page 238) made up to step 5	
1 x	recipe	Mayonnaise Colée (see page 19)	
200g	8oz	ham (12 slices)	
250ml	½ pint	double cream	
	1tsp	horseradish	grated
	8 half	walnuts	skinned
5g	¼oz	fresh parsley	washed

Method

1 Line a small Charlotte mould with half the aspic.
2 Bind the Salade Waldorf with the Mayonnaise Colée, pour it into the Charlotte mould and smooth the top level.
3 MIRROR A FLAT with the rest of the aspic.
4 Cut the ham into ovals and, using a cream horn tin as a mould, roll the ham round it to form cornets.
5 Mix the cream and horseradish together well and fill the cornets with it, then decorate 8 of them with walnuts and 4 with the parsley.

Service

Dip the Charlotte mould into very hot water for a few seconds then unmould the Salade Waldorf carefully onto the centre of the mirrored FLAT. Place the cornets of ham garnished with the walnuts around the base of the Salade and the cornets garnished with the parsley on the top of it.

Uses

Table d'hôte hors-d'oeuvres.

Cornets/Roulade de Jambon Garnis

CORNETS/ROULADE FILLED WITH PÂTÉ OR CREAM CHEESE AND GARNISHED

Portions: 4

Quantity		Ingredients	Preparation
100g	4oz	ham or smoked ham	sliced
50g	2oz	pâté *or* cream cheese	cream
	2	stuffed olives	sliced
100g	4oz	pineapple	peeled and cored

Method

Cornets
1 Cut the sliced ham into ovals.
2 Using a cream horn tin as a mould, roll the ham round it to form cornets.
3 Pipe with the pâté or cream cheese.
4 Decorate as required.

Roulade
1 Pipe the filling over the slices of ham.
2 Roll the ham into a cylinder.
3 Decorate.

Service

Serve in a RAVIER dish, garnished with the stuffed olive slices and pineapple.

Uses
Hors-d'oeuvre varié.

Darioles de Foie Gras

DARIOLES OF PÂTÉ WITH ASPIC

Portions: 4

Quantity		Ingredients	Preparation
500ml	1 pint	aspic (see page 4)	
125ml	¼ pint	egg whites	
	1	truffle	drained and finely diced or cut into julienne
400g	1lb	pâté de foie gras	
	1	salad	

Method

1 Put 8 small dariole moulds in the freezer, until they are very cold (about an hour).
2 Carefully melt the aspic.
3 Line the dariole moulds with half the aspic.
4 Strain the egg whites into a buttered ovenproof dish, cover with buttered paper and cook gently in a bain-marie until set, then leave to cool. Cut into shapes required.
5 Decorate the prepared dariole moulds with the truffle and cut poached egg white.
6 Cream the pâté de foie gras until it is smooth, then spoon it into a piping bag.

7 Pipe the pâté carefully into the prepared moulds.
8 Cover with the remaining aspic.
9 Leave to set.
10 Dip the darioles into very hot water for a few seconds then turn out carefully onto the serving plates or FLAT.

Service

Serve with the salad.

Uses

Single cold hors-d'oeuvres.

Fonds d'Artichaut Farcis

STUFFED ARTICHOKE BOTTOMS

Portions: 4

Quantity		Ingredients	Preparation
	1 tin	artichoke bottoms	drained
50g	2oz	butter	softened
200g	½lb	smooth pâté	sieved
125ml	5fl oz	cream	
100g	4oz	button mushrooms	TURNED
	1	lemon	juiced
250ml	½ pint	aspic (see page 4)	

Method

1 Trim the artichoke bottoms with a fluted cutter.
2 Beat the butter until smooth.
3 Add the pâté and cream together.
4 Add the cream and beat together until the mixture has a smooth texture.
5 Cook the mushrooms in water with the lemon juice to keep them white.
6 Spoon the pâté mixture into a piping bag with a star nozzle.
7 Pipe the mixture onto the centre of the artichoke until it has domed.
8 Place the mushrooms on top.
9 Put them on a cooling rack.
10 NAPPER with the aspic as it is just beginning to set to glaze them.

Service

When the aspic has set, slice the finished artichoke bottoms from the cooling rack, lift them carefully and put them on a RAVIER dish.

Uses

Hors-d'oeuvre varié.

Fromage Blanc aux Herbes

CREAM CHEESE WITH HERBS

Yield: 500ml (1 pint)

Quantity		Ingredients	Preparation
395g	14oz	cream cheese	
	4tbsp	double cream	
	1tbsp	wine vinegar	
	2tbsp	walnut oil	
	1tbsp	fresh parsley	chopped
	1tbsp	fresh chervil	chopped
	1tsp	shallots	finely chopped
		salt and pepper	

Method

1 Put all the ingredients into a bowl.
2 Season with salt and pepper.
3 Whisk together thoroughly.
4 Chill.

Variations

Service

Serve in small pots.

Derivatives

Uses

For Petite Corbeille de Cruditées (see page 100).

Gelée de Cassis à la Russe

BEETROOT AND BLACKCURRANT JELLY WITH SOUR CREAM

Portions: 6

Quantity		Ingredients
Beetroot and blackcurrant jelly		
	5	baby beetroots
500ml	1 pint	blackcurrant juice
10g	½oz	gelatine
	2tbsp	port
125ml	¼ pint	sour cream
	2tsp	lime juice
Cornets		
	12	slices smoked ham
150g	6oz	cream cheese

Method

1 Lightly oil 6 120ml (4fl oz) jelly moulds.
2 Slice 4 of the baby beetroots thinly and divide them between the moulds, lining them.
3 Cut the remaining beetroot into thin sticks and reserve.
4 Bring the blackcurrant juice to the boil, remove it from the heat, add the gelatine, wait until it has dissolved, then add the port.
5 Fill the prepared moulds with the jelly and leave to set for about 2 hours.
6 Unmould the jellies by dipping the moulds into hot water for a few seconds then carefully turning them out onto the serving plate.
7 Add the lime juice to the cream and whisk gently until it is thick.
8 Make the ham into cornets by wrapping the trimmed slices around a cream horn tin.
9 Spoon the cream cheese into a piping bag and fill the ham cornets.

Service

Serve the jellies with the filled ham cornets, the soured cream spooned onto each plate and garnish with the reserved thin sticks of beetroot.

Variations

_____

_____

_____

Uses

_____

_____

_____

Derivatives

_____

_____

_____

Jambon de Parme aux Figues

PARMA HAM WITH FIGS

Portions: 4

Quantity	Ingredients	Preparation
150g 6oz	parma ham	sliced thinly
¼ tin *or* 4 fresh	figs	drain, if tinned; clean and halve if fresh

Method

1 Trim the ham.

Service

Wrap the ham around the figs and place neatly on a serving plate.

Jambon Fumé aux Pêches

SMOKED HAM WITH PEACHES

Portions: 4

Quantity		Ingredients
200g	8oz	sliced smoked ham
	2	peaches
	8 sprigs	watercress
1 x	recipe	Sauce Oxford (see page 26)

Method

1 Make the ham into cornets by wrapping it around a cream horn tin, allowing 3 cornets per portion.
2 Halve the peaches lengthways then slice thinly, stopping short of one end, to form fans.
3 Wash and trim the watercress.
4 Make Sauce Oxford as given in the recipe and leave to cool.

Service

Place three cornets of ham on each plate at the top and a peach fan slightly overlapping the ends of the cornets. Place watercress inside each cornet, then pour a CORDON of Sauce Oxford around the edge of each plate.

Uses

Variations

Derivatives

Legumes à la Grecque

GREEK-STYLE VEGETABLES

Portions: 4

Quantity		Ingredients	Preparation
500ml	1 pint	water	
125ml	¼ pint	oil	
	1	lemon	juiced
	1 sprig	thyme	
	1	bay leaf	
	6	peppercorns	
	pinch	salt	
400g	1lb	celery *or*	
		cauliflower *or*	
		mushrooms *or*	
		fennel *or*	
		pickling onions	
Garnish			
	1 sprig	thyme	
	1	bay leaf	

Method

1 Prepare the vegetables: cut celery into batons, cauliflower into florets, trim and TURN the mushrooms, peel and cut the fennel into wedges, or peel the onions.
2 Mix all the ingredients together in a saucepan.
3 Bring to the boil.
4 Simmer gently.
5 Cook the vegetables until *al dente* (just cooked, not soft).
6 Leave to cool.

NB: Fennel and celery seeds may also be used.

Service

Serve in a RAVIER dish, NAPPER with
the cooking liquor and garnish with
the thyme and bay leaf.

Uses

Hors-d'oeuvre varié.

Legumes à la Portugaise

PORTUGUESE-STYLE VEGETABLES

Portions: 4

Quantity		Ingredients	Preparation
400g	1lb	onions *or* pickling onions *or* button mushrooms *or* cauliflower	finely chopped *or* peeled
	1 clove	garlic	finely chopped
125ml	¼ pint	oil	
400g	1lb	tomatoes	made into a CONCASSER
100/125g	4–5oz	tomato purée	
	1 sprig	thyme	
	1	bay leaf	
125ml	¼ pint	white stock	
		salt and pepper	
Variations:			
400g	1lb	button mushrooms *or* cauliflower	washed, trimmed and TURNED *or* cut into florets

Method

1 Sweat the onions and garlic in the oil until cooked.
2 Add the tomato CONCASSER and cook until soft.
3 Add the tomato purée, which will give it a lovely colour.
4 Add the herbs and stock and season to taste.
5 If using, add the mushrooms *or* florets and simmer in the sauce until *al dente* (just cooked, not soft).

Service

Leave to cool until cold, then spoon the vegetables into a RAVIER and NAPPER with the sauce.

Uses

Hors-d'oeuvre varié.

Mortadella

Portions: 4

Quantity	Ingredients	Preparation
100g 4oz	Mortadella	thinly sliced
Garnish		
2	dill pickles	
1 bunch	watercress	washed, dried and trimmed

Method

1 Fold the Mortadella slices in half or form into cornets using a cream horn tin as a mould.
2 Cut the dill pickles in half on the diagonal and slice thinly to form a fan.

Service

Arrange the Mortadella decoratively on the plate. Garnish with the dill pickle fans and the watercress.

Uses

Table d'hôte single hors-d'oeuvres.

Mousse Appareil

BASIC MOUSSE

Portions: 4

Quantity		Ingredients	Preparation
125ml	¼ pint	velouté	
100g	4oz	filling (e.g., prawns, chicken, ham)	liquidised and sieved
	6 leaves	gelatine	soaked in cold water
		salt and pepper	
125ml	¼ pint	double cream	lightly whipped

Method

1 Heat the velouté and add the filling.
2 Drain the gelatine, add it to the mixture and stir until the gelatine has melted.
3 Put the pan on some ice and leave to cool until it begins to set.
4 Fold in the cream.
5 Pour the mousse into moulds and chill until set (about an hour).

Service

Dip the moulds momentarily into very hot water, lay the serving plate over the mould, quickly invert, give the mould a sharp tap and carefully lift the mould off.

Mousse d'Artichaut

ARTICHOKE MOUSSE

Portions: 4

Quantity		Ingredients	Preparation
	3 large	artichoke bottoms	cooked
	2 leaves	gelatine	soaked in cold water
	1tbsp	white wine	
125ml	5fl oz	double cream	lightly whipped
		salt and pepper	

Method

1 Liquidise the artichoke bottoms in a food processor or blender.
2 Add the gelatine to the wine and heat gently until the gelatine has melted.
3 Stir the artichoke purée into the wine and gelatine mixture.
4 Leave the mixture to cool on ice until it has almost set.
5 Fold in the cream.
6 Season to taste.
7 Spoon into 4 small moulds and chill until the mousse has set.

Service

For each mousse, dip the mould into hot water for a few seconds, place the serving plate on top, invert, give the mould a sharp tap, then carefully lift the mould off. Serve with Asparagus and Tomato Mousses (see pages 79 and 88).

Uses

Single hors-d'oeuvres.

Mousse d'Asperge

ASPARAGUS MOUSSE

Portions: 4

Quantity		Ingredients	Preparation
250g	10oz	asparagus	cooked and refreshed
	2 leaves	gelatine	soaked in cold water
	1tbsp	sherry	
125ml	5fl oz	double cream	lightly whipped
		salt and pepper	

Method

1 Liquidise the asparagus, reserving a few to use as a garnish, and pass it through a fine sieve to produce a smooth purée.
2 When the gelatine has softened, melt it in a tablespoonful of very hot water.
3 Stir in the sherry and the asparagus purée.
4 Leave the mixture to cool on ice until it has almost set.
5 Fold in half of the cream.
6 Season to taste.
7 Chill until set (about 1–2 hours) and then, using a wetted dessertspoon, form the mousse into quennels on the serving plates.

Service

Serve with a suitable sauce (mayonnaise- or vinaigrette-based), garnished with the reserved asparagus spears.

Uses

Single hors-d'oeuvres.

Mousse de Bouquet

MINIATURE PRAWN MOUSSE

Portions: 4

Quantity		Ingredients	Preparation
125ml	5fl oz	*court bouillon* (see page 2) *or* chicken stock	
10g	½oz	butter	
10g	½oz	flour	
200g	8oz	peeled prawns	coarsely chopped
	1½tsp	powdered gelatine	
	2½tbsp	dry white wine	
125ml	5fl oz	mayonnaise	
	2tbsp	tomato purée	
	¼tsp	tabasco sauce	
		salt and pepper	
75ml	2½fl oz	double cream	lightly whipped
Garnish			
	1	avocado	peeled, stoned and sliced
	4	lettuce leaves	washed
	4	unshelled prawns	peel the shell off the body only
	4 small sprigs	dill (optional)	

Method

1 Make a velouté sauce with the butter, flour and stock, cooking it gently for 20 minutes.
2 Add the prawns and leave to cool.
3 Sprinkle the gelatine over the wine in a small pan, then dissolve the gelatine over heat.

4 Stir the gelatine and wine mixture into the sauce with the mayonnaise, tomato purée and tabasco, and season to taste.
5 Fold in the cream, pour the mixture into 4 moulds and chill until set (about an hour).

Service

For each mousse, dip the mould
in hot water for a few seconds,
put the serving plate over the top,
invert, give the mould a sharp tap
and lift it off. Then garnish with
the slices of avocado, lettuce
leaves, prawns and a sprig of dill,
if using.

Uses

_____

_____

_____

Variations

_____

_____

_____

Derivatives

_____

_____

_____

Mousse de Concombre à la Menthe

MINTED CUCUMBER MOUSSE

Portions: 4

Quantity		Ingredients	Preparation
	4	cucumbers	peeled and diced
50g	2oz	gelatine	
500ml	1 pint	white chicken stock	heated through
	2 bunches	mint	washed
	4tbsp	white wine *or* cider vinegar	
	5tsp	castor sugar	
	1 pinch	ground coriander *or* mace	
400g	1lb	cream cheese	
1 litre	2 pints	double cream	lightly whipped
	2	egg whites	whipped until forms stiff peaks

Method

1 Place the cucumber in a sieve, sprinkle with salt and leave to stand for 30 minutes.
2 Dissolve the gelatine in the hot stock, then leave until it is cold.
3 Chop some of the mint leaves.
4 Rinse and dry the cucumber, then mix it with the chopped mint, vinegar, sugar and coriander or mace.

5 Beat the cucumber mixture into the cream cheese, together with the gelatine and stock mixture.
6 Leave until the mixture just begins to set.
7 Fold the cream into the mousse.
8 Fold the egg whites into the mousse.
9 Pour the mousse into 4 small ring moulds and chill until it is set (about an hour).

Service

For each mousse, dip the moulds in hot water for a few seconds, place the serving plate on top, invert, give the mould a sharp tap, then carefully lift the mould off. Fill the centres with the remaining mint leaves.

Uses

Variations

Derivatives

Mousse de Foie de Volaille

CHICKEN LIVER MOUSSE

Portions: 4

Quantity		Ingredients	Preparation
125ml	¼ pint	velouté	
100g	4oz	chicken liver pâté	sieved
	6 leaves	gelatine	soaked in cold water
		salt and pepper	
125ml	¼ pint	double cream	lightly whipped
500ml	1 pint	aspic (see page 4)	
25g	1oz	garnishing paste	

Method

1 Heat the velouté and mix in the pâté.
2 Drain the gelatine and stir until it has melted.
3 Leave the pan to cool over ice until the sauce and pâté mixture begins to set.
4 Fold in the cream.
5 Pour the mousse into 4 small soufflé dishes, smooth the top level and chill until set (about an hour).
6 Then dip each mould into hot water for a few seconds and turn out onto a wire cooling rack. Coat with a thin layer of aspic.
7 Decorate with the garnishing paste and cover with aspic again.

Service

Serve each mousse on a water-lily serviette (handle them carefully when lifting them off the wire rack, trimming off any rough edges).

Uses

Single, cold hors-d'oeuvres.

Mousse de Jambon
HAM MOUSSE

Portions: 4

Quantity		Ingredients	Preparation
125ml	¼ pint	velouté	
100g	4oz	lean ham	liquidised and sieved
	6 leaves	gelatine	soaked in cold water
		salt and pepper	
125ml	¼ pint	double cream	lightly whipped
500ml	1 pint	aspic (see page 4)	
Garnish			
50g	2oz	ham	sliced

Method

1 Heat the velouté through and add the ham.
2 Drain the soaked gelatine and stir it into the velouté and ham mixture until it has melted and season.
3 Leave the pan to cool over ice until the mixture begins to set.
4 Fold the cream into the mixture.
5 Pour the mousse into 4 ramekin dishes or small soufflé dishes and chill until set (about an hour).
6 When set, glaze the top with the aspic.
7 Form the ham into cornets by wrapping it around a cream horn tin.
8 Spoon the remaining mousse into the ham cornets.

Service

Serve each mousse on a water-lily serviette with a filled ham cornet on the top.

Uses

Single, cold hors-d'oeuvres.

Mousse de Poivrons Rouges

PEPPER MOUSSE WITH TOMATO SAUCE

Portions: 8

Quantity		Ingredients	Preparation
Mousse			
10g	½oz	onion	finely chopped
	2tbsp	olive oil	
	3	medium tomatoes	made into a CONCASSER
	3	red peppers	finely chop 2¾ peppers; cut remainder into fine julienne
	2½ leaves	gelatine	
120ml	4fl oz	white wine vinegar	
	1tsp	raspberry vinegar	
	½tsp	cayenne pepper	
		salt	
375ml	16fl oz	whipping cream	
Tomato coulis			
	10	tomatoes	made into a CONCASSER
	1tbsp	tomato purée	
	2tbsp	white wine vinegar	
	3tbsp	olive oil	
	1 pinch	sugar	
		black pepper	
Jelly (optional)			
	2 leaves	gelatine	
200ml	8fl oz	water	
	½	red pepper	cut into fine dice

Method

1 First make the mousse. Sweat the onion in the olive oil for 1 minute.
2 Add the tomato CONCASSER and chopped peppers and cook for 10 minutes, stirring the mixture well.
3 Soak the gelatine in water for 10 minutes.
4 Reduce the white wine vinegar to a third of its volume, then add the onion, tomato and pepper mixture.
5 Stir in the raspberry vinegar, gelatine, cayenne pepper and salt.
6 Liquidise the mixture in a food processor or blender and pass through a sieve into a bowl.
7 Leave to cool until tepid, then whip the cream and mix a quarter of it into the purée.
8 Fold in the remaining cream and adjust the seasoning, if necessary.
9 Pour the mousse into a terrine or 8 small moulds and chill until set (about an hour).
10 Next, make the tomato coulis. Liquidise the tomato CONCASSER, purée and white wine vinegar in a food processor or blender, then slowly add the olive oil.
11 Pass through a fine sieve and season to taste with the sugar and black pepper.
12 Now make the jelly, if using. Soak the gelatine in warm water for 10 minutes.
13 Bring the water to the boil and dissolve the gelatine in it.
14 Mix the pepper with the jelly.
15 Cool the mixture over ice until it has almost set.
16 Briefly dip the tureen or each mould into hot water, put a plate over the top, invert, give the mould a sharp tap and carefully lift off the mould, then pour the jelly evenly over each one.

Service

Cut the mousse into slices and place them on the serving plate(s). NAPPER the plate with a CORDON of the tomato coulis and garnish with the julienned pepper.

Uses

_____

_____

_____

Variations

Make three mousses, each using red or green or yellow peppers and serve one slice of each colour to each person (use small individual moulds to set the mousses in) for Bavarois de Poivrons Trois Colors.

Derivatives

_____

_____

_____

Mousse de Tomate

TOMATO MOUSSE

Portions: 4

Quantity		Ingredients	Preparation
1⅛l	2¼ pints	aspic (see page 4)	
100g	4oz	tomatoes	made into a CONCASSER
25g	1oz	butter	
125ml	¼ pint	velouté	
	1tsp	tomato purée	
	6 leaves	gelatine	soaked in cold water
		salt and pepper	
125ml	¼ pint	double cream	lightly whipped
Garnish			
	4	medium tomatoes	blanched, skinned and hollowed out
10g	½oz	garnishing paste	

Method

1 Line 4 dariole moulds with 500ml (1 pint) aspic between them and chill until set (about 1-2 hours).
2 Meanwhile, sweat the tomato concasser in the butter for 4–5 minutes and add the tomato purée.
3 Process the cooked concasser in a food processor or blender.
4 Pass through a fine sieve to remove any remaining lumps or pips.
5 Heat the velouté, add the tomato mixture, season and mix together well.

6 Drain the gelatine and melt it in the velouté mixture.
7 Leave the pan to cool over ice until it starts to set.
8 Fold in the cream.
9 Pour the mousse into the aspic-lined dariole moulds and chill until set.
10 Fill the hollowed out tomatoes with the remaining mousse, cut a wedge out of each, glaze with a little aspic and leave to set over ice for about 15-20 minutes.
11 Set the remaining aspic on a FLAT dish and, when set, cut into diamonds.

Service

Dip the dariole moulds briefly in hot water and turn out quickly onto a MIRRORED FLAT. Decorate with diamonds of aspic. Place a filled tomato next to each mousse with its wedge next to it and decorate with the garnishing paste as required.

Uses

Single, cold hors-d'oeuvres.

Oeufs de Caille Froid au Cresson

QUAILS' EGGS WITH WATERCRESS

Portions: 4

Quantity	Ingredients	Preparation
20	quails' eggs	
Garnish:		
2 bunches	watercress	washed, dried and trimmed

Method

1 Hard-boil the quails' eggs for 8–10 minutes, run cold water over them until they are cold, then remove the shells.

Service

Arrange the watercress on 4 serving plates in 'nest' shapes. Place 5 eggs in the middle of each nest. Serve with a suitable sauce such as Mayonnaise or Thousand Island Dressing (see pages 18 and 38).

Uses

Cold, single hors-d'oeuvres.

Oeufs Durs Froid Moscovite

EGGS STUFFED WITH CAVIAR AND ARTICHOKE BOTTOMS

Portions: 4

Quantity		Ingredients	Preparation
	4	eggs	hard-boiled
	4	artichoke bottoms	trimmed
50g	2oz	black mock caviar	
	4	anchovy fillets	drained
	1 slice	garnishing paste	thinly sliced
500ml	1 pint	aspic (see page 4).	

Method

1 Run cold water over the eggs until they are cold, then remove their shells.
2 Trim the bottoms from the eggs.
3 Remove the yolk from the middle using a column cutter.
4 Fill the centres with the caviar.
5 Stand the eggs on the trimmed artichoke bottoms.
6 Decorate the eggs with strips of anchovy fillets, like the rings on a barrel, and place a disc of garnishing paste on top for a bung.
7 Glaze with aspic and leave to set.
8 MIRROR A FLAT with aspic.
9 Set the remaining aspic and chop it neatly.

Service

Place a ring of chopped aspic around the centre of the FLAT. Put the decorated eggs together in the middle.

Uses

Table d'hôte hors-d'oeuvres.

Oeufs en Gelée

EGGS IN ASPIC

Portions: 4

Quantity		Ingredients	Preparation
750ml	1½ pint	aspic (see page 4)	
5g	¼oz	garnishing paste	sliced thinly
	4	eggs	poached

Method

1 Line 4 oval moulds with 250ml (½ pint) aspic.
2 Decorate neatly with the garnishing paste.
3 Refresh the eggs and trim neatly.
4 Place the eggs into the moulds and fill the spaces with 250ml (½ pint) aspic.
5 MIRROR A FLAT with 250ml (½ pint) aspic.
6 Set the remaining aspic and chop it up neatly.

Service

Dip the mould in hot water and unmould carefully onto the mirrored flat, then decorate round it neatly with the chopped aspic.

Uses

Table d'hôte hors-d'oeuvres.

Oeufs Farcis

STUFFED EGGS

Portions: 4

Quantity		Ingredients	Preparation
	4	eggs	hard-boiled
25g	1oz	butter	softened
125ml	¼ pint	mayonnaise	
		salt and pepper	
Garnish			
	4–8	capers	drained
	½	lettuce	washed and dried

Method

1 When the eggs are cooked, run cold water over them until they are cold, then remove the shells.
2 Cut the eggs in half lengthways or leave whole and VAN DYKE the top.
3 Remove the yolks and sieve them.
4 Put the butter into a bowl, add the egg yolks and cream them together.
5 Add the mayonnaise and cream and season to taste.
6 Spoon the mixture into a piping bag with a star nozzle.
7 Pipe the filling back into the egg whites.

Service

Put a caper on top of the piped egg yolk mixture in each egg and place on a bed of lettuce.

Uses

Table d'hôte hors-d'oeuvres.

Variations

Add tomato, anchovy *or* spinach purée to the yolk for different colours. Use a suitable garnish for each.

Oeufs Mayonnaise

EGGS COATED IN MAYONNAISE

Portions: 4

Quantity		Ingredients	Preparation
	4	eggs	hard-boiled
	1	lettuce	washed and dried
250ml	½ pint	mayonnaise	
	¼tsp	paprika	
	4	anchovy fillets	drained and cut into strips
	4	capers	drained

Method

1 Run cold water over the eggs until they are cold, then remove their shells.
2 Cut them into slices, halves or wedges.
3 CHIFFONADE the lettuce finely.
4 Thin the mayonnaise to coating consistency with a tablespoonful of hot water and mix in the paprika.

Service

Either on a plate, or a RAVIER, make a bed of the lettuce over the bottom, arrange the egg on top and coat with the mayonnaise. Decorate as required.

Uses

Table d'hôte single hors-d'oeuvres or hors-d'oeuvre varié.

Oeufs Poché en Gelée Fruits de Mer

POACHED EGGS IN ASPIC WITH SEAFOOD

Portions: 4

Quantity		Ingredients	Preparation
1l	2 pints	aspic (see page 4)	
5g	¼oz	truffle	
5g	¼oz	red pimento	cut into diamonds
	6	eggs	poached
50g	2oz	cooked lobster	SALPICON
50g	2oz	peeled prawns	
50g	2oz	poached scallops	SALPICON
50g	2oz	poached scampi	SALPICON
Garnish			
	4	crayfish	brush with oil and SET THE CLAWS

Method

1 Line a savarin mould with 250ml (½ pint) aspic and leave to set.
2 Decorate the top with truffle and diamonds of red pimento.
3 Refresh the eggs and trim to a neat shape.
4 Place the eggs in the mould, pour in 250ml (½ pint) aspic and leave to set.
5 Mix the seafood together and spoon evenly into the savarin.
6 Pour in 250ml (½ pint) aspic and leave to set.
7 MIRROR A FLAT with 250ml (½ pint) aspic.

8 Set the remaining aspic in a thick layer on a flat plate, then cut it into 'croûtons'.

Service

Dip the savarin mould into hot water for a moment then carefully unmould it on to the mirrored flat. Decorate with the crayfish and aspic croûtons.

Uses

Table d'hôte hors-d'oeuvres.

Oeufs Poches Froid Alexander

POACHED EGG TARTS WITH CHAUFROID SAUCE AND ASPIC

Portions: 4

Quantity		Ingredients	Preparation
	6	eggs	poached
250ml	½ pint	sauce chaufroid	
	2 slices	truffle	
750ml	1½ pints	aspic (see page 4)	
	4	tartlet cases	baked blind
50g	2oz	black caviar	

Method

1 Refresh the eggs and trim to a good shape.
2 Place them on a cooling rack and coat with the chaufroid sauce.
3 Decorate with a piece of the truffle.
4 Glaze with 250ml (½ pint) of the aspic and leave to set.
5 Trim when set.
6 Put equal amounts of caviar in each of the tartlet cases.
7 Place the eggs in the tartlet cases.
8 MIRROR A FLAT with 250ml (½ pint) of the aspic.
9 Set the remaining aspic and cut it into 'croûtons'.

Service

Place the egg tartlets on the flat and garnish with the aspic croûtons.

Uses

Table d'hôte hors-d'oeuvres.

Pastrami Salad

Portions: 4

Quantity		Ingredients	Preparation
200g	8oz	pastrami	thinly sliced
	1	red pepper	
	1	green pepper	
	1	yellow pepper	
	1	salad as required	

Method

1 Cut the peppers in half lengthways.
2 Remove the cores, seeds and white from the middle.
3 Quarter the peppers, then cut into a fine julienne.

Uses

Table d'hôte hors-d'oeuvres.

Service

Arrange the peppers and salad decoratively in the centre of a serving plate. Neatly place the thinly sliced Pastrami around the salad.

Oeufs Poches Froids Frou-frou

POACHED EGGS WITH
CHAUFROID SAUCE AND
ASPIC WITH GLAZED
MAYONNAISE AND
VEGETABLE TERRINE

Portions: 4

Quantity		Ingredients	Preparation
1l	2 pints	aspic (see page 4)	
100g	4oz	petits pois	cooked, refreshed and drained
100g	4oz	French beans	cooked refreshed and cut into lozenges
100g	4oz	asparagus spears	cooked, refreshed and diced
½ x	recipe	mayonnaise colée (see page 19)	
	6	eggs	poached
250ml	½ pint	sauce chaufroid	
	1	egg	hard-boiled and sieved
	4 slices	truffle	

Method

1 Line a small Charlotte mould with 250ml (½ pint) aspic and leave to set (15–20 minutes).
2 Mix the vegetables together and mix in the Mayonnaise Colée.
3 Pour the vegetable mixture into the prepared mould, level the top and leave to set.
4 Refresh the eggs and trim them to neaten.
5 Place the eggs on a cooling rack.
6 Coat them with the sauce chaufroid.
7 Decorate each with the sieved egg yolk and white and truffle slices.
8 Glaze them with 250ml (½ pint) of the aspic and when it has set (it takes about 15–20 minutes), trim the edges.

9 MIRROR A FLAT with 250ml (½ pint) of the aspic.

10 Set the remaining aspic and chop it up neatly.

Service

Dip the Charlotte mould in hot water and unmould the vegetable terrine carefully in the centre of the flat. Surround it with the eggs and garnish with the chopped aspic.

Uses

Table d'hôte hors-d'oeuvres.

Petite Corbeille de Cruditées avec Trois Sauces

BASKET OF CRUDITÉS WITH DIPS

Portions: 4

Quantity		Ingredients	Preparation
100g	4oz	carrot	cut into short, thickish julienne
100g	4oz	celery	cut into short, thickish julienne
100g	4oz	red pepper	cut into short, thickish julienne
100g	4oz	cucumber	cut into short, thickish julienne
100g	4oz	spring onions	
	1	oak leaf lettuce	
	1	endive	
	1	radicchio	
1 x	recipe	Anchovy Dip (see page 55)	
1 x	recipe	Sauce Rouille (see page 120)	
1 x	recipe	Fromage Blanc aux Herbes (see page 68)	

Method

1 Keep the vegetables crisp in the fridge.
2 Wash and dry the salad leaves.
3 Prepare the dips as given in the recipes.

Service

Arrange the vegetables on a bed of salad leaves and serve with the dips.

Variations

Other vegetables that also make excellent crudités are: cauliflower florets, avocado slices, red cabbage, celeriac, chicory, fennel, button mushrooms and radishes or blanched vegetables, including French beans, broccoli florets, courgettes, mange-tout and asparagus.

Poire d'Avocat au Stilton

AVOCADO WITH STILTON

Portions: 4

Quantity		Ingredients	Preparation
	2	avocados	halved and stones removed
	1	lemon	juiced
200g	8oz	Stilton cheese	
125ml	¼ pint	double cream	
	1	lettuce	washed and dried
	¼	cucumber	grooves cut along it with a CANELLE KNIFE and thinly sliced

Method

1 Cut the flesh in a trellis pattern all the way through the flesh but without cutting through the skin.
2 Rub the flesh with the lemon juice to stop it discolouring.
3 Cut the Stilton into 16 small diamonds and reserve these for later.
4 Finely sieve the remaining cheese.
5 Cream the cheese and cream together to a piping consistency.
6 Spoon it into a piping bag with a star nozzle.
7 Pipe rosettes of cheese in the hole left by the stone.
8 Decorate the rosettes with the diamonds of Stilton.

Service

Serve each finished avocado half on a bed of lettuce, garnished with the cucumber.

Uses

Single hors-d'oeuvres.

Poire d'Avocat avec Cresson et Sauce Fraises

AVOCADO AND WATERCRESS WITH STRAWBERRY SAUCE

Portions: 4

Quantity	Ingredients	Preparation
2	avocados	halved and stones removed
1	lemon	juiced
Dressing		
3tbsp	natural yogurt	
1tbsp	white wine	
2tbsp	strawberry purée	
Garnish		
4	strawberries	halved
4 small bunches	watercress	washed and trimmed

Method

1 Slice the avocado halves thinly, stopping just short of one end to form a fan.
2 NAPPER with the lemon juice.
3 Prepare the dressing by mixing the yogurt, wine and strawberry purée together.

Service

NAPPER each serving plate with the dressing, then place the avocado fan in the centre and decorate with the small bunches of watercress and half strawberries.

Uses

Variations

Derivatives

Poire d'Avocat avec Crevettes

AVOCADO WITH PRAWNS

Portions: 4

Quantity		Ingredients	Preparation
	2	ripe avocados	halved and stones removed
	1	lemon	juiced
200g	8oz	peeled prawns	
	8	unshelled prawns	peel the shell off the body only
5g	¼oz	mock caviar	
	1	lettuce	washed and dried
½ x	recipe	Sauce Marie Rose (see page 28)	

Method

1 Cut the avocado flesh in a trellis pattern all the way through the flesh but without cutting through the skin.
2 Rub the flesh with the lemon juice to stop discolouration.
3 Fill the hole left by the stone with the peeled prawns.
4 Decorate the top with two of the part-peeled prawns and a quarter of the mock caviar.

Service

Make a bed of lettuce on each serving plate and place the avocados on top. Serve a sauce-boat of the Sauce Marie Rose separately.

Uses

Single hors-d'oeuvres.

Poire d'Avocat avec Fruits de Mer

SEAFOOD AVOCADO

Portions: 2

Quantity		Ingredients	Preparation
	I	ripe avocado	halved and stone removed
	½	lemon	juiced
100g	4oz	white crab meat	
		salt and pepper	
	6	unshelled prawns	
½ x	recipe	Sauce Marie Rose (see page 28)	
	2 PLUCE	fresh parsley	washed

Method

1 Slice the avocado halves thinly lengthways, stopping short of cutting through at one end to form a fan.
2 NAPPER with the lemon juice.
3 Flake the crab meat and season.
4 Shell just the tails of the prawns, leaving the heads attached.

Service

NAPPER each serving plate with the Sauce Marie Rose and place an avocado fan in the centre. Place a small BOUQUET of crab meat on either side of the pear at the top, place 3 of the prawns in the middle and a little parsley on the crab meat.

Uses

Variations

Derivatives

Poire d'Avocat Bon Viveur

AVOCADO WITH CELERY, CHEESE AND ROQUEFORT DRESSING

Portions: 2

Quantity		Ingredients	Preparation
	1	avocado	halved, stone removed and skinned
	½	lemon	juiced
	1	stick celery	cut into short julienne
50g	2oz	Roquefort cheese	finely grated
Roquefort dressing			
60ml	2fl oz	vinegar	
120ml	4fl oz	olive oil	
		fresh parsley	chopped
		fresh chives	chopped
		fresh tarragon	chopped
		fresh chervil	chopped
100g	4oz	Roquefort cheese	finely grated
		green peppercorns	
		salt and pepper	
Garnish			
	¼ bunch	watercress	washed and trimmed

Method

1 Slice the avocado halves thinly lengthways, not cutting all the way through at one end, and fan out.
2 NAPPER with the lemon juice.
3 Whisk the dressing ingredients together and season with salt and pepper.

Service

Place each avocado fan in the centre of a plate, pile the celery neatly at the top, NAPPER with the dressing and place a BOUQUET of cheese on either side. Garnish with the watercress.

Uses

Derivatives

Variations

Poire d'Avocat Epicure

STUFFED AVOCADO

Portions: 4

Quantity		Ingredients	Preparation
	2	avocados	halved and stones removed
10g	½oz	walnuts	skinned and chopped
250ml	½ pint	mayonnaise	
	4	walnut halves	
	4	pickled walnuts	drained and sliced
5g	¼oz	fresh parsley	washed
	1	lettuce	wahed and dried
	2	lemons	1 cut into wedges, 1 juiced

Method

1 Cut the avocado flesh into a trellis pattern all the way through the flesh but without cutting through the skin.
2 Rub with the lemon juice to stop it discolouring.
3 Remove the flesh carefully with a spoon and put it into a bowl reserving the 'shells'.
4 Mix the flesh carefully together with the walnuts and mayonnaise.
5 Spoon the mixture back into the avocado shells, slightly doming it.
6 Decorate the top with the half walnuts, slices of pickled walnut and the parsley.

Service

Serve each avocado half on a bed of lettuce with wedges of lemon.

Uses

Single hors-d'oeuvres.

Poire d'Avocat Singapour

AVOCADO WITH CRAB AND MAYONNAISE

Portions: 4

Quantity		Ingredients	Preparation
	2	avocados	halved and stones removed
	1	lemon	juiced
100g	4oz	white crab meat	flaked and seasoned
125ml	¼ pint	mayonnaise	
5g	¼oz	fresh parsley	washed
	1	lettuce	washed and dried
	¼	cucumber	grooves cut along it with a CANELLE KNIFE and thinly sliced

Method

1 Cut the avocado flesh in a trellis pattern all the way through the flesh but without cutting through the skin.
2 Rub the flesh with the lemon juice to stop it discolouring.
3 Fill the holes left by the stones with the white crab meat, saving a little for garnishing.
4 NAPPER the crab meat with the mayonnaise.
5 Decorate each with a BOUQUET of crab meat and parsley.

Service

Serve each of the finished avocado halves on a bed of lettuce, garnished with the slices of cucumber.

Uses

Single hors-d'oeuvres.

Poire d'Avocat Vinaigrette

AVOCADO WITH VINAIGRETTE

Portions: 4

Quantity		Ingredients	Preparation
	2	avocados	halved and stones removed
	1	lemon	juiced
	1	lettuce	washed and dried
250ml	½ pint	vinaigrette	

Method

1 Cut the avocado flesh in a trellis pattern all the way through the flesh but without cutting through the skin.
2 Press the skin with your fingers to dent it so that it will not rock when placed on the plate.
3 Rub the flesh with the lemon juice to stop it discolouring.

Service

Make a bed of lettuce on each serving plate and place the prepared avocado halves in the middle. Serve the vinaigrette separately in a sauce-boat.

Uses

Single hors-d'oeuvres.

Poivrons Macerer

MARINATED PEPPERS

Portions: 4

Quantity		Ingredients	Preparation
	1	red pepper	blanched and skinned
	1	green pepper	blanched and skinned
	1	yellow pepper	blanched and skinned
250ml	½ pint	olive oil	
	2 clove	garlic	finely crushed
		salt and pepper	

Method

1 Cut the peppers into quarters, remove the seeds and trim.
2 Place in a clean jar.
3 Mix the oil and garlic and season.
4 Pour the flavoured oil over the peppers and shake to ensure that they are well covered.
5 Seal the jar and store for 3–5 days before use, shaking the jar from time to time.

Service

Drain the peppers, slice the lemon into fine julienne and mix them together well.

Uses

As required, but ideal as a simple salad.

Poivrons Provençale

PROVENÇALE PEPPERS

Portions: 4

Quantity		Ingredients	Preparation
	¼tsp	fennel seeds	
	¼tsp	celery seeds	
	¼tsp	coriander seeds	
	¼tsp	black peppercorns	
500ml	1 pint	water	
125ml	¼ pint	olive oil	
	1	lemon	juiced
	1 sprig	thyme	
	1	bay leaf	
	2	red peppers	cut into julienne
	1	green pepper	cut into julienne
	1	yellow pepper	cut into julienne
300g	12oz	tomatoes	made into a CONCASSER
Garnish			
	1 sprig	thyme	
	1	bay leaf	

Method

1 Add the fennel, celery and coriander seeds and the peppercorns to the water, oil, lemon juice, thyme and bay leaf in a sauté pan.
2 Bring to the boil and simmer.
3 Cook the peppers in the à la Grecque mixture.
4 When cooked, add the tomato CONCASSER.
5 Leave to cool.

Service

Carefully spoon the mixture into a RAVIER dish and shape as required, garnishing with the sprig of thyme and bay leaf.

Use

Table d'hôte vegetable hors-d'oeuvres or as an hors-d'oeuvre varié.

Rillettes de Porc

POTTED PORK

Portions: 10

Quantity		Ingredients	Preparation
2kg	4lb	belly pork	
1½kg	3lb	fat bacon	
	2	bay leaves	
	1 sprig	thyme	
100g	4oz	onions	chopped
		salt and pepper	
200g	8oz	lard	melted
5g	¼oz	parsley	washed

Method

1 Carefully prepare the pork by de-boning it, removing the rind, removing all the sinew and cutting into dice.
2 Cut the fat bacon into dice.
3 Place the bay leaves, thyme and onion into a muslin bag and tie.
4 Place the pork, bacon and bouquet garni in a pan and cover.
5 Cook in a bain-marie with the water boiling.
6 Cook until the meat is golden in colour (for about 30 minutes).
7 Remove the herbs.
8 Leave the mixture to cool.
9 Pass the meat through the fine plate of a mincer or pound in a mortar. (If minced, pass it through a fine sieve.)
10 Season to taste.
11 Spoon the mixture into 10 china ramekins and smooth the top level.
12 Pour the melted lard over the top of each one – just enough to cover the top completely and seal it.

Service

Serve either on a serving dish on a water-lily serviette or on a FLAT on DISH PAPER, garnished with the parsley.

Uses

Table d'hôte hors-d'oeuvres.

Rosette Saucisson

ROSETTE WITH SALADS

Portions: 4

Quantity		Ingredients	Preparation
200g	8oz	Rosette saucisson	thinly sliced
	1	salad	
150g	6oz	tomatoes	blanched and skinned
150g	6oz	Potato Salad (see page 223)	

Method

1 Remove the skin from the Rosette saucisson and trim where necessary.
2 Cut the tomatoes into wedges or slice them.

Uses

Table d'hôte hors-d'oeuvres.

Service

Arrange the salad in the middle of the serving plate, leaving a margin around the edge. Decorate the middle with the potato salad and tomatoes, then make a border round the edge of the plate by slightly overlapping the slices of Rosette saucisson.

Salade de Mange-tout au Gingembre

MANGE-TOUT SALAD WITH GINGER AND MINT DRESSING

Portions: 4

Quantity		Ingredients	Preparation
10g	½oz	root ginger	
	2tbsp	wine vinegar	
	1tbsp	castor sugar	
		salt and pepper	
400g	1lb	mange-tout	
	4tbsp	oil	
25g	1oz	mint leaves	shredded
	12	quails' eggs	
	4	tartlet cases	
50g	1oz	black mock caviar	

Method

1 Peel and grate or cut the root ginger into fine julienne, putting a little to one side to use later.
2 Heat the wine vinegar and pour it over the ginger and castor sugar in a bowl and leave it to cool. Then season with salt and pepper.
3 Toss and rub the mange-tout with a few drops of the oil, then steam them with the reserved ginger until *al dente* (just cooked, not soft).

4 Refresh the cooked mange-tout with cold water, then drain well.
5 Turn them in the vinegar and ginger mixture, toss well, add the remaining oil and the mint, then leave to marinate for 10 minutes.
6 Meanwhile, hard-boil the quails' eggs for 10 minutes, run cold water over them until they are cool, then remove the shells.

Service

Place equal amounts of the mange-tout salad neatly in a ring on each of the 4 serving plates. Divide the black caviar equally between the tartlet cases, place 3 quails' eggs on top of the caviar in each case and put each finished tartlet in the middle of the salad.

Uses

Variations

Derivatives

Salade de Topinambours Vinaigrette

BEAN AND JERUSALEM ARTICHOKE SALAD

Portions: 4

Quantity		Ingredients	Preparation
400g	1lb	French green beans	
400g	1lb	Jerusalem artichokes	
		salt and pepper	
Vinaigrette			
250ml	½ pint	hazelnut oil	
250ml	½ pint	groundnut oil	
250ml	½ pint	white wine vinegar	
Garnish			
		assorted lettuce leaves	washed, dried and trimmed
		chervil	

Method

1 Top and tail the beans and steam or blanch them for 3–4 minutes, then refresh and drain well.
2 Wash the Jerusalem artichokes, trim off any knobbly bits, peel and slice them into medium-thick rounds. Season and steam for 5–7 minutes until tender.
3 Make the vinaigrette by mixing all the ingredients together well and season to taste.

Service

Toss the warm Jerusalem artichokes in three-quarters of the vinaigrette. Arrange equal amounts of the salad leaves on each of the 4 plates and pile up equal amounts of the Jerusalem artichokes in the centre of each one. Toss the beans in the remaining vinaigrette and then scatter them around the pyramids.

Uses

_____

_____

_____

Derivatives

_____

_____

_____

Variations

_____

_____

_____

Salade de Trois Poivrons et Jambon

THREE PEPPER SALAD WITH HAM

Portions: 4

Quantity	Ingredients	Preparation
1	red pepper	blanched and skinned
1	green pepper	blanched and skinned
1	yellow pepper	blanched and skinned
1	oak leaf lettuce	washed and dried
150g 6oz	Parma ham	thinly sliced

Method

1 Cut each pepper in half lengthways, remove the core, seeds and ribs.
2 Quarter the peppers, then cut them into fine julienne.
3 Trim the oak leaf lettuce as necessary.
4 Trim the ham if required.

Uses

Single hors-d'oeuvres.

Service

Arrange the lettuce and peppers decoratively in the middle of a serving plate, leaving a margin around the outside. Then arrange the Parma ham slices neatly around the salad.

Salami de Milan

ITALIAN SALAMI WITH WATERCRESS AND GHERKIN

Portions: 4

Quantity	Ingredients	Preparation
100g 4oz	Italian salami	thinly sliced
1 bunch	watercress	washed and dried
4	gherkins	

Method

1 Remove the skin from the salami.
2 Trim the watercress.
3 Slice each gherkin thinly, stopping short of one end to make a fan.

Service

Arrange equal amounts of the salami decoratively on 4 serving plates and garnish each with the watercress and a gherkin fan.

Uses

Table d'hôte single hors-d'oeuvres.

Sauce Rouille

DIP FOR CRUDITÉS

Yield: 500ml (1 pint)

Quantity	Ingredients	Preparation
3	hard-boiled egg yolks	
2	egg yolks	
1 clove	garlic	finely chopped
1tsp	tomato purée	
½tsp	ground ginger	
1	lemon	juiced
1 pinch	saffron	
1½tsp	Dijon mustard	
½tsp	cayenne pepper	
125ml 6fl oz	oil	

Method

1 Put all the ingredients except the oil in a food processor or blender.
2 Process until smooth.
3 Gradually add the oil until the sauce thickens.

Service

Serve in small pots.

Uses

For Petite Corbeille de Cruditées (see page 100).

Variations

Derivatives

Tomatoes à la Monegasque

TOMATOES WITH TUNA MAYONNAISE STUFFING

Portions: 4

Quantity		Ingredients	Preparation
	8	medium tomatoes	blanched and skinned
250ml	½ pint	vinaigrette	
200g	8oz	tuna fish	drained and sieved
25g	1oz	onions	finely chopped
	½tsp	fresh parsley	finely chopped
	½tsp	fresh chervil	finely chopped
	½tsp	fresh tarragon	finely chopped
	2	eggs	hard-boiled and seived
125ml	¼ pint	mayonnaise	
25g	1oz	butter	softened
	1	lettuce	washed and dried
	¼	cucumber	grooves cut along it with a CANELLE KNIFE and thinly sliced

Method

1 Remove the tops from the tomatoes (reserving them) and spoon out and discard the seeds.
2 Fill each with vinaigrette and leave to marinate for 4–5 minutes.
3 Mix the sieved tuna fish, onions, herbs (reserving a little parsley), egg (reserving a little) and mayonnaise together well.
4 Spoon the tuna mixture into a piping bag.
5 Drain the vinaigrette from the tomatoes and brush the outsides with it.
6 Pipe the tuna mixture into the tomatoes.
7 Decorate the top with the reserved egg and parsley.
8 Replace the lids and pipe with butter in the shape of leaves.

Service

Place the finished tomatoes (2 per person) on beds of lettuce, garnished with the cucumber.

Uses

Single hors-d'oeuvres.

Tomates Sevigne

TOMATOES WITH CHICKEN MAYONNAISE STUFFING

Portions: 4

Quantity		Ingredients	Preparation
	8	tomatoes	blanched and skinned
125g	5oz	chicken SUPREME	cooked
		salt and pepper	
250ml	½ pint	mayonnaise	
	1 bunch	chervil	finely chopped
125ml	¼ pint	vinaigrette	
	1	green pepper	finely diced
	1	lettuce	washed and dried

Method

1 Slice off the bottoms of the tomatoes and reserve.
2 Carefully spoon out and discard the seeds.
3 Finely dice the cooked supreme of chicken.
4 Mix the chicken, chervil and mayonnaise together and season to taste.
5 Carefully spoon the chicken mayonnaise into the tomatoes.
6 Brush the tomatoes with the vinaigrette.
7 Top each with the diced green pepper.
8 Replace the lid, setting it at an angle.

Service

Arrange the leaves from the heart of the lettuce on a white, oval SUR LE PLAT DISH. Place the finished tomatoes on top.

Uses

Table d'hôte hors-d'oeuvres.

Westphalaine Mettwurst

SAUSAGE WITH PEPPERS AND POTATO SALAD

Portions: 4

Quantity		Ingredients	Preparation
	1	green pepper	cut into julienne
	1	red pepper	cut into julienne
	1	yellow pepper	cut into julienne
	1	black pepper	cut into julienne
200g	8oz	Continental sausage	thinly sliced
	1	curly endive	washed and dried
150g	6oz	potato salad	

Method

1 Cut the peppers in half lengthways, remove the core, seeds and ribs.
2 Quarter them, then cut them into fine julienne.
3 Remove the skin from the sausage slices, if necessary.

Use

Table d'hôte vegetable hors-d'oeuvres.

Service

Arrange the curly endive on a serving plate, followed by the potato salad and peppers. Then place the sausage decoratively on the plate.

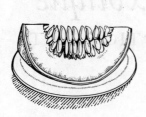

5
FRUIT HORS-D'OEUVRES

Assiette Exotique
Assiette Miami
Assiette Surprise
Cocktail à l'Espagnole
Cocktail/Coupe Florida
   Cocktail/Coupe Hawaii
   Cocktail/Coupe Miami
   Cocktail/Coupe d'Orange
   Cocktail de Deux Pamplemousse
   Cocktail de Pamplemousse
Cocktail de Fruit Frais
Cocktail de Melon aux Trois
  Colors
Cocktail de Melon et Fraise
   Cocktail de Melon et Framboise
   Cocktail de Melon et Gingembre
   Cocktail de Melon Menthe
   Cocktail de Melon aux Porto

Delice des Tropiques
Demi Pamplemousse Cerisette
  Demi Pamplemousse
  Demi Pamplemousse au Kirsch
Jus d'Ananas Frais
  Jus d'Orange Frais
  Jus de Pamplemousse Frais
Gelée de Mangues avec Jambon et
  Sauce aux Framboises
Mangue Frappé
Melon à l'Americaine
Melon d'Israel au Porto
Melon Surprise
Melon Victoria
Papaya Frappé
Tranche d'Ananas Frais Hawaii
Tranche de Melon Frappé

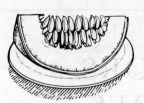

Assiette Exotique
PLATE OF EXOTIC FRUITS

Portions: 8

Quantity		Ingredients	Preparation
½x	recipe	Coulis de Framboise et Fraise (see page 12)	
	4	kiwi fruit	peeled and sliced
	4	star fruits	sliced
	1 punnet	strawberries	hulled and washed
	1	Ogen melon	flesh sliced
400g	1lb	kumquats	
	6	pink grapefruits	segmented
	6	limes	sliced *or* segmented
	2	red apples	cored and sliced
	2	green apples	cored and sliced
	4	lemons	
1½kg	3lb	cranberries	
25g	1oz	fresh mint leaves	
	1	fig	

Method

1 Prepare all the fruits carefully and use only the best quality fresh fruits.

Service

Just before serving, NAPPER the serving plate with the strawberry and raspberry sauce then carefully place the fruits onto the plate in colour and texture sequence.

Uses

Variations

Use any seasonal fruits that are available.

Derivations

_____

_____

_____

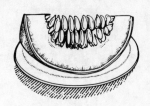

Assiette Miami

PLATE OF ORANGE AND PINEAPPLE

Portions:

Quantity	Ingredients	Preparation
1	orange	
1	pineapple	peel and core removed

Method

1 Cut the orange zest into fine julienne, blanch and refresh them.
2 Slice the top and bottom off the orange, cutting between the pith and the flesh.
3 Cut the orange in half, carefully loosen the segments from the skin with a curved knife, then separate the segments from each other by slicing as close as you can to each side of the membrane. Lift them out of the skin.
4 Squeeze the juice from the flesh remaining attached to the membranes.

Service

Arrange the pineapple rings in a circle around the centre of the serving plate, fan the orange segments around the inside of the circle, NAPPER with the orange juice, then place the zest decoratively around the outside of the circle of pineapple.

Uses

Variations

Derivatives

Cocktail/Coupe Hawaii (see page 132).

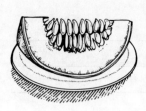

Assiette Surprise

MELON AND FRUITED CREAM CHEESE WITH BLACKCURRANT COULIS

Portions: 4

Quantity		Ingredients
	1	Ogen melon
50g	2oz	kiwi fruit
50g	2oz	passion fruit
50g	2oz	strawberries
150g	6oz	cream cheese
Blackcurrant coulis		
200g	8oz	blackcurrants
50g	2oz	sugar
Garnish		
25g	1oz	mint leaves

Method

1 Skin the melon and cut the flesh into slices, each about 1cm (⅜in) thick.
2 Make individual purées from each of the fruits.
3 Divide the cream cheese into thirds, putting each third in its own bowl, put 1 of the 3 fruit purées into each bowl and mix well together.
4 Shape each of the fruited cream cheese mixtures into quenelles using two wetted dessertspoons (make 4 from each flavour).
5 Make a blackcurrant coulis using the method for Coulis de Fraise (see page 11).
6 Chill for about an hour before serving.

Service

Coat each serving plate with blackcurrant coulis. Place a slice of melon on one side of the plate and garnish with the mint leaves. Place 2 quenelles of each fruit flavour on the other half of the plate. Chill well for about an hour before serving.

Variations

Use any other suitable combinations
of fruit, the colours and flavours of
which go well together.

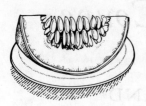

Cocktail à l'Espagnole
SPANISH COCKTAIL

Portions: 4

Quantity		Ingredients
	2 measures	brandy
	4	unshelled prawns
	1	Honeydew melon
100g	4oz	peeled prawns
250ml	½ pint	thick mayonnaise
25g	1oz	red or black mock caviar

Method

1 Cut the melon in half lengthways, remove the seeds, cut the flesh into balls, using a PARISIENNE CUTTER (number 25–26) and marinate in the brandy.
2 Remove the melon flesh that remains and chop it finely.
3 Peel the shells from bodies of the prawns, leaving the heads attached.

Service

Place the melon balls around the outside of a wide champagne glass or shallow glass dish and fill the centre with the chopped melon. Arrange the peeled prawns on top and pipe a rosette of thick mayonnaise around them. Decorate with the semi-peeled prawns and caviar.

Uses

Variations

Derivatives

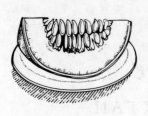

Cocktail/Coupe Florida

GRAPEFRUIT AND ORANGE COCKTAIL

Portions: 4

Quantity	Ingredients	Preparation
4	large grapefruits	
4	large oranges	
4	maraschino cherries	drained

Method

1 Prepare the grapefruits as given for the orange on page 128, putting the segments and juice into a bowl.
2 Prepare the oranges in the same way.

Service

Place the segments in 4 shallow glass dishes, overlapping them alternately. NAPPER with the juice. Decorate each dish with a cherry.

Uses

Single cold hors-d'oeuvres.

Variations

As above, but pile diced pineapple (total of 100g/4oz) in the middle for a Cocktail/Coupe Hawaii.
As above, but use 8 oranges and replace the grapefruit with 100g (4oz) pineapple for a Cocktail/Coupe Miami.
As above, but make with just oranges (8) for a Cocktail/Coupe d'Orange.
As above, but make with 4 grapefruits and 4 pink grapefruits for Cocktail de Deux Pamplemousse.
As above but just one type of grapefruit (4) for a Cocktail de Pamplemousse.

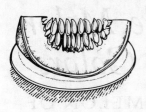

Cocktail de Fruits Frais

FRESH FRUIT COCKTAIL

Portions: 4

Quantity		Ingredients	Preparation
	1	Ogen melon	
	1 punnet	strawberries	hulled and washed
50g	2oz	black grapes	separated and washed
50g	2oz	kumquats	cleaned
	1	kiwi fruit	peeled and diced
100g	4oz	pineapple	peeled, cored and diced
	1	star fruit	sliced
	1	papaya	peeled, de-seeded and diced
50ml	2fl oz	kirsch	
	1 bunch	mint	leaves removed and washed

Method

1 Cut the melon in half lengthways, remove the seeds, cut the flesh into balls, using a PARISIENNE CUTTER (number 25–26).
2 Remove the remaining melon flesh and chop it finely.
3 Cut the strawberries into halves, or quarters if large.
4 Cut the grapes in half and remove the seeds.
5 Remove the stalks from the kumquats.

Service

Place the fruit decoratively in a wide champagne glass or shallow glass dish. NAPPER with the kirsch to moisten, decorate with the mint leaves and chill for about an hour. Serve on a DISH PAPER on a FLAT or doily on a side plate.

Uses

Fruit hors-d'oeuvres.

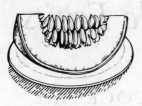

Cocktail de Melon aux Trois Colors

COCKTAIL OF MELON OF THREE COLOURS

Portions: 4

Quantity		Ingredients
	1	honeydew melon
50ml	⅛ pint	port
50ml	⅛ pint	crème de menthe
50ml	⅛ pint	kirsch

Method

1 Top and tail the melon.
2 Cut it in half lengthways and remove the seeds.
3 Cut the flesh into balls, using a PARISIENNE CUTTER (number 25–26).
4 Put equal numbers of melon balls into 3 bowls – one containing the port, one the crème de menthe and the third, the kirsch – and leave to marinate for about an hour.

Service

Place the marinated melon balls in 4 goblets or wide champagne glasses, putting those soaked in port at the bottom, those in crème de menthe in the middle and those in kirsch on top. Chill for about an hour. Then serve on FLATS with DISH PAPER or side plates with doilies.

Uses

Cold single hors-d'oeuvres.

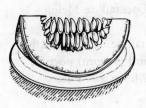

Cocktail de Melon et Fraise

COCKTAIL OF MELON AND STRAWBERRIES

Portions: 4

Quantity		Ingredients	Preparation
1		honeydew melon	
50g	2oz	strawberries	hulled and washed
50ml	⅛ pint	kirsch	

Method

1 Top and tail the melon.
2 Cut it in half lengthways and remove the seeds.
3 Cut the flesh into balls using a PARISIENNE CUTTER (number 25–26).
4 Place the balls in a container.
5 Slice the remaining flesh from the skin and chop it finely.

Service

Place the chopped melon in 4 shallow glass dishes, goblets or wide champagne glasses. Put the melon balls around the chopped melon and the strawberries in the middle, then chill for about an hour. NAPPER with kirsch just before serving on a FLAT with DISH PAPER or side plates with doilies.

Uses

Cold, single hors-d'oeuvres.

Variations

As above but replace the strawberries with the same amount of raspberries for Cocktail de Melon et Framboise.
As above but melon on its own, piling the melon balls neatly over the chopped melon, for Cocktail de Melon Frappé.
As above but replace the strawberries and kirsch with 5g (¼oz) sliced stem ginger, piling the melon balls neatly over the chopped melon and placing the ginger on top for Cocktail de Melon et Gingembre.
As above but marinate the melon

balls in 25ml (¼ pint) crème de menthe, dome the balls over the chopped melon and decorate with mint leaves and pour any remaining crème de menthe over just before serving for Cocktail de Melon Menthe.

As for Cocktail de Melon Menthe but with 125ml (¼ pint) port for Cocktail de Melon aux Porto.

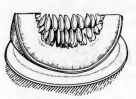

Delice des Tropiques

TROPICAL FRUITS WITH YOGURT

Portions: 4

Quantity		Ingredients	
125ml	¼ pint	natural yogurt	
	4	kiwi fruits	
	1	pineapple	
	1	avocado	
	1	lemon	juiced

Method

1 Neatly peel and slice the kiwi fruit.
2 Peel the pineapple, cut into quarters, remove the centre core, then slice the flesh into thin triangles.
3 Cut the avocado in half lengthways, remove the stone and skin.
4 Cut the avocado halves in half and thinly slice each quarter, stopping short of one end to form a fan.
5 NAPPER the avocado fans with the lemon juice to stop them discolouring.

Service

NAPPER each plate with the natural yogurt. Then arrange the fruit on each plate as follows. Down the middle, place pineapple triangles, overlapping them. Down one side place overlapping slices of kiwi fruit. On the other side, place an avocado fan.

Uses

Cold hors-d'oeuvres.

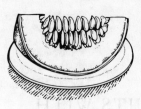

Demi Pamplemousse Cerisette

HALF GRAPEFRUITS WITH CHERRIES

Portions: 4

Quantity	Ingredients	Preparation
6	large grapefruits	
4	maraschino cherries	drained

Method

1 Cut 2 of the grapefruits in half (through the equator) and remove any seeds.
2 Neatly cut the skin in a zig zag pattern along the edge and cut each segment free (see page 128).
3 Release them at the bottom and remove them.
4 Peel the remaining grapefruits and break up into segments.
5 Place thin segments of grapefruit on the top of each half.
6 NAPPER with grapefruit juice to moisten.
7 Place a cherry in the middle of each grapefruit half.

Service

Serve each grapefruit half in shallow glass dishes on DISH PAPER and FLATS or on side plates and doilies.

Uses

Cold, single hors-d'oeuvres.

Variations

As above but without cherries for a simple Demi Pamplemousse.
As above but NAPPER the grapefruit halves with 75ml (⅛ pint) kirsch for Demi Pamplemousse au Kirsch.

Jus d'Ananas Frais

FRESH PINEAPPLE JUICE

Yield: 500ml (1 pint)

Quantity		Ingredients	Preparation
50g	2oz	castor sugar	
250ml	½ pint	water	
	1	pineapple	peeled, cored and diced

Method

1 Place the sugar and water in a pan and bring to the boil.
2 Leave to go cold.
3 Place the diced pineapple in a liquidiser or blender and process with the stock syrup until smooth.
4 Adjust the quantity of stock syrup used depending on the sweetness of the pineapple.
5 Strain and chill.
6 Strain through a CHINOIS before using.

Service

Serve chilled, either in a glass jug or in goblets.

Uses

Table d'hôte hors-d'oeuvre and for breakfasts.

Variations

As above but replace the pineapple with 6 large oranges for Jus d'Orange Frais.

As above but replace the pineapple with 6 large grapefruits for Jus de Pamplemousse Frais.

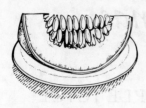

Gelée de Mangues avec Jambon et Sauce aux Framboises

MANGO JELLY WITH SMOKED HAM AND REDCURRANT SAUCE

Portions: 4

Quantity		Ingredients	Preparation
Mango jelly			
	2	ripe mangoes	peeled
	3	oranges	juiced
10g	½oz	gelatine	
Redcurrant coulis			
200g	8oz	redcurrants	
50g	2oz	sugar	
100g	4oz	smoked ham	

Method

1 Purée the mango flesh with the orange juice.
2 Reserve 4 tablespoons of the purée and add the gelatine to the remainder.
3 Gently heat until the gelatine dissolves.
4 Pour the purée into 6 75ml (3fl oz) moulds and chill in the fridge until it has set (about an hour).

5 Next, make the redcurrant coulis. Place the redcurrants and sugar into a pan with 2 tablespoons of water.
6 Cook over a gentle heat until the fruit starts to burst.
7 Adjust the taste, if necessary, with sugar, depending on the tartness or sweetness of the redcurrants, pass through a sieve and chill for about an hour.

8 Form the ham into cornets using
  a cream horn tin to shape them.

Service

Dip the moulds in hot water for a
few seconds then carefully turn each
mango jelly out onto a serving plate
and pour a little of the reserved
mango purée over each jelly. Put
the cornets of smoked ham by the
jellies. Serve the redcurrant coulis
separately.

Uses

_____

_____

_____

Variations

Can be served without the smoked
ham.
Other fresh fruits may also be used,
such as, kiwi, peach or melon.

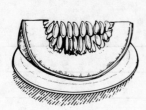

Mangue Frappé
CHILLED MANGO

Portions: 4

Quantity	Ingredients
3	mangoes

Method

1 Cut each of the mangoes in half lengthways.
2 Twist the halves to separate them.
3 Remove the stones.
4 Remove the flesh from the skins, keeping the flesh and skins of 4 of the halves whole.
5 Slice the flesh and replace it neatly in 4 of the halves.
6 Decorate the top with the slices from the third mango.

Service

Serve on a DISH PAPER and FLAT or individual plates.

Uses

Cold, single hors-d'oeuvres.

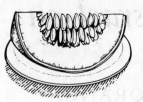

Melon à l'Americaine

MELON WITH SAUCE

Portions: 4

Quantity		Ingredients	Preparation
	1	Honeydew melon	
	4	oranges	juiced
75ml	2fl oz	brandy	
150ml	4fl oz	tomato ketchup	

Method

1 Top and tail the melon.
2 Cut in half lengthways and remove the seeds.
3 Cut the flesh into balls using a PARISIENNE CUTTER (number 25–26).
4 Remove the remaining melon flesh and chop it finely.
5 Mix the orange juice with the brandy and tomato ketchup to make a sauce.

Service

Place the finely chopped melon in 4 shallow glass dishes or PARISIENNE GOBLETS and surround it with the melon balls, placing them neatly. NAPPER with the sauce. Serve on DISH PAPER on a FLAT or doily on a side plate.

Uses

Cold, single hors-d'oeuvres.

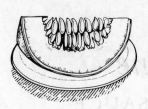

Melon d'Israel au Porto

MELON WITH ORANGE AND PORT

Portions: 4

Quantity		Ingredients	Preparation
	4	small Ogen melons	
125ml	¼ pint	port	
	1	orange	
	4	maraschino cherries	drained

Method

1 VAN DYKE the top of the melons and remove them.
2 Carefully remove the seeds from inside.
3 Pour the port into the melons.
4 Invert the tops and put them back onto the melons.
5 Use a CANELLE KNIFE to cut grooves into the orange skin before cutting it into thin slices.
6 Cut each of the 4 orange slices from the centre to the outside and twist into cornets.
7 Place a cornet on each melon lid.
8 Garnish each of the orange cornets with a cherry in the middle.

Service

Serve the melons in shallow glass dishes or, if too large, on crushed ice.

Uses

Cold, single hors-d'oeuvres.

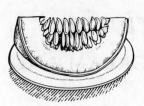

Melon Surprise

MELON WITH LAYERED FRUITS

Portions: 4

Quantity	Ingredients
2	Ogen melons
4	large oranges
½	pineapple
4	kiwi fruits
1 punnet	strawberries

Method

1 Cut the melons in half by cutting them VAN DYKE style around their equators and remove the seeds.

2 Cut the melon flesh into balls using a PARISIENNE CUTTER (number 25–26).

3 Remove the remaining melon flesh and chop it finely. Reserve the melon skin 'shells'.

4 Peel and core the pineapple, cut it into wedges and then slice to form triangles.

5 Peel and segment (see page 128) the oranges, freeing them from skin, pith, peel and seeds.

6 Peel the kiwi fruits and slice them thinly.

7 Hull and wash the strawberries.

8 Place some of the chopped melon in the bottom of each of the reserved skins.

9 Place the melon balls in a ring around the inside edge of the melon skins.

10 Place the orange segments in a ring inside the orange ring.

11 Place the pineapple triangles inside the orange ring.

12 Place the kiwi fruit slices overlapping in a ring inside the pineapple triangles ring.

13 Finish by putting the strawberries in a group in the centre.

Service

Serve each finished melon in a shallow glass dish on crushed ice.

Uses

Cold, single hors-d'oeuvres.

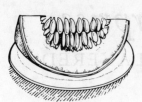

Melon Victoria

MELON WITH CREAM AND GINGER

Portions: 4

Quantity	Ingredients	Preparation
250ml ½ pint	whipping cream	whipped
½tsp	ground ginger	
1 large	Honeydew melon	
1 piece	crystallised ginger	

Method

1 Fold the ground ginger into the whipped cream and spoon it into a piping bag with a star-shaped nozzle.
2 Cut the melon in half lengthways and remove the seeds.
3 Cut the melon flesh into balls using a PARISIENNE CUTTER (number 25–26).
4 Finely chop the crystallised ginger.

Service

Arrange the melon balls in 4 PARISIENNE GOBLETS. Pipe a rosette of ginger cream on top of the melon balls in each goblet. Arrange the chopped ginger decoratively on top of the cream.

Uses

Variations

Mix the cream with the melon balls instead of piping it on top, then put them into the goblets.

Derivatives

Papaya Frappé

PAPAYA WITH STRAWBERRY COULIS

Portions: 4

Quantity		Ingredients	Preparation
200g	8oz	frozen strawberries	
	1	lemon	juiced
10g	½oz	castor sugar	
	2	papayas	peeled, halved and de-seeded
	4	strawberries	hulled and washed
	1oz	mint	leaves picked off stems, stems discarded, leaves washed and dried

Method

1 Liquidise the frozen strawberries in a food processor or blender.
2 Pass the purée through a CHINOIS to remove any lumps.
3 Add lemon juice and sugar to taste.
4 Slice the papaya halves thinly lengthways or cut in thin slices stopping just short of one end to form a fan.
5 Cut the strawberries into halves or quarters, depending on their size.

Service

NAPPER 4 serving plates with the strawberry coulis. Place the papaya slices or fans in the centre of each plate, then garnish with the mint leaves and strawberries.

Uses

Cold, single fruit hors-d'oeuvres.

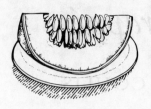

Tranche d'Ananas Frais Hawaii

SLICED PINEAPPLE BOAT

Portions: 4

Quantity Ingredients

1	pineapple
4	large oranges
4	grapefruits

Method

1 Remove a thin slice from the bottom of the pineapple.
2 Cut it into 4 wedges.
3 Remove the central core.
4 Release the flesh from the skin, leaving it attached at each end.
5 Cut the flesh into thin slices.
6 Remove the zest from the oranges and cut it into thin julienne, blanch and refresh until cold.
7 Peel the oranges, separate them into segments and squeeze the juice from half of them.
8 Peel the grapefruits and separate them into segments.

Service

Place a sliced pineapple wedge in the middle of each of the 4 serving plates. For each one, place orange segments overlapping down one side and grapefruit segments down the other. Garnish with the orange zest julienne and NAPPER with the orange juice.

Uses

Cold, single hors-d'oeuvres.

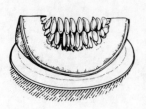

Tranche de Melon Frappé

SLICED MELON BOAT

Portions: 4

Quantity	Ingredients	Preparation
1	large Honeydew melon	
1	orange	
4	maraschino cherries	drained

Method

1 Top and tail the melon and cut in half lengthways.
2 Carefully remove the seeds.
3 Cut each half in half to make quarters.
4 Remove a thin slice of skin along the centre so that the melon wedge will not rock.
5 Release the flesh from the skin, leaving it attached at each end.
6 Cut the flesh into thin slices.
7 Use a CANELLE KNIFE to cut grooves into the orange skin before cutting it into thin slices.
8 Thread an orange slice onto a cocktail stick, and a cherry on top. Make 4 the same.

Service

Push the slices of melon along each wedge, one to the left, one to the right. Place an orange 'sail' in the middle of each wedge and serve on a FLAT with DISH PAPER or individual serving plates.

Uses

Cold, single hors-d'oeuvres.

Tranche de Melon
Frappé

SLICED MELON BOAT

Use

6
FISH AND SEAFOOD HORS-D'OEUVRES

Terrine de Fruits de Mer

Terrine de Poisson

   Turbon de Poisson avec Coulis de
   Tomate

Terrine de Poisson

Timbale de Saumon Fumé

Tomates avec Crevettes

Truite Fumé avec Sauce Raifort

Truite Mariné

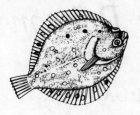

Assiette de Fruits de Mer

SEAFOOD PLATTER

Portions: 4

Quantity		Ingredients	Preparation
200g	8oz	mussels	shells removed
100g	4oz	smoked mackerel	
	1	salad (any type)	
50g	2oz	peeled prawns	
50g	2oz	cockles	drained
	1 tin	sardines	drained

Garnish

To complement salad chosen.

Method

1 Skin the mackerel and cut it into SUPREMES and lightly brush with oil.

Service

Arrange the salad in the middle of a clean serving plate. Then, surround the salad with the fish and shellfish, arranging it attractively, and garnish suitably.

Uses

Table d'hôte hors-d'oeuvres.

Assiette de Poisson Fumé

SMOKED FISH PLATTER

Portions: 4

Quantity		Ingredients	Preparation
100g	4oz	smoked trout	
100g	4oz	smoked eel	
100g	4oz	smoked mackerel	
50g	2oz	smoked salmon	
		oil	
	1	lettuce	washed and dried
	1	lemon	cut into wedges
	¼	cucumber	grooves cut along it with a CANELLE KNIFE and thinly sliced

Method

1 Skin and fillet the smoked trout and cut it into SUPREMES.
2 Skin and fillet the smoked eel or cut it into DARNES.
3 Skin and fillet the smoked mackerel and cut it into SUPREMES.
4 Slice the smoked salmon thinly and roll them into roulades or cornets.
5 Lightly brush the fish with oil.

Service

Arrange the fish decoratively on a bed of lettuce on a serving dish. Garnish with the wedges of lemon and the cucumber. Serve a suitable sauce separately.

Uses

Cold, single hors-d'oeuvres.

Assiette Méli-melo

WHITE AND GREEN ASPARAGUS SALAD WITH SCALLOPS

Portions: 4

Quantity		Ingredients	Preparation
	6	white asparagus tips	
	16	green asparagus tips	
	12	fresh scallops	
	1	carrot	peeled
	4tbsp	natural yogurt	
	½	lemon	juiced
		salt and pepper	
50g	2oz	lettuce heart	
50g	2oz	oak leaf lettuce heart	
50g	2oz	leaves of curly endive	
	1tsp	olive oil	
	4 sprigs	chervil	

Method

1 Cook the asparagus, refresh and cover.
2 Slice the scallops.
3 Use a CANELLE KNIFE to cut grooves along the carrot, then slice it thinly and blanch for 1 minute in boiling water.
4 Mix the yogurt and lemon juice together and season to taste.
5 Arrange the salad leaves, asparagus and carrots on 4 plates and spoon the yogurt over them.
6 Sauté the scallop corals quickly in the olive oil for 15 seconds, add the scallop slices and sauté for a further 15 seconds, then season to taste.

Service

Put the cooked scallops on top of the salads and garnish each plate with a sprig of chervil.

Variations

Bouquets en Cascade

CASCADE OF PRAWNS WITH GARLIC MAYONNAISE

Portions: 4

Quantity		Ingredients	Preparation
200g	8oz	unshelled prawns	defrosted
	¼	cucumber	grooves cut along it with a CANELLE KNIFE and thinly sliced
	1	lemon	
½ x	recipe	Sauce Aïoli (see page 23)	
	1	lettuce	washed and dried

Method

1 Set the prawns on a SILVER CASCADE.
2 Cut each of the cucumber slices from the centre out and twist.
3 Top and tail the lemon, cut in half, then into wedges.
4 Remove the centre core and any seeds and place each wedge into a lemon squeezer (where available).
5 Spoon Sauce Aïoli into a piping bag with a star nozzle and pipe into a sauce-boat.

Service

Make a bed of lettuce on a FLAT, then place the cascade of prawns in the middle. Garnish with the cucumber twists, lemon wedges and rosettes of piped Sauce Aïoli. Serve a sauce-boat of Sauce Aïoli separately.

Uses

Cold single hors-d'oeuvres.

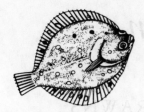

Cocktail de Crabe
CRAB COCKTAIL

Portions: 4

Quantity	Ingredients	Preparation
1	lettuce	washed and dried
200g 8oz	white crab meat	flaked and seasoned
1	lemon	grooves cut along it with a CANELLE KNIFE, cut into wedges and pith removed from centre
½ x recipe	Sauce Marie Rose (see page 28)	
Optional garnishes		
	crab *or* lobster coral	
	mock caviar, black *or* red	
	sieved hard-boiled egg	
	paprika	
	chopped parsley	
	tomato roses	

Method

1 Finely CHIFFONADE the lettuce and arrange in the bottom of 4 shallow glass dishes or wide champagne glasses.
2 Place the flaked white crab meat on top.
3 NAPPER with the Sauce Marie Rose.

Service

Garnish with one or more of the optional garnishes, then put the dishes on DISH PAPER on FLATS or doilies on side plates.

Uses

Cold, single hors-d'oeuvres.

Cocktail de Crevettes Indienne

PRAWN COCKTAIL WITH CURRY SAUCE

Portions: 4

Quantity		Ingredients	Preparation
	1	lettuce	washed and dried
200g	8oz	peeled prawns	
5g	¼oz	butter	
5g	¼oz	curry powder	
	1tbsp	mango chutney	
½ x	recipe	Sauce Marie Rose (see page 28)	
100g	4oz	tomatoes	blanched and skinned
	1	egg	hard-boiled and shelled
	8	prawns	peel the shell from the body only

Method

1 Finely CHIFFONADE the lettuce and arrange in the bottom of 4 shallow glass dishes or wide champagne glasses.
2 Place the peeled prawns on top.
3 Melt the butter and gently cook the curry powder in it for a minute.
4 Finely chop the mango chutney.
5 Mix the curry powder and chutney with the Sauce Marie Rose.
6 NAPPER the prepared prawns and lettuce with the Sauce Marie Rose mixture.

7 Cut the tomatoes into wedges.
8 Cut the egg into wedges.

Service

Garnish by putting some of the part-peeled prawns on the centre of each dish and the tomato and egg wedges on the sides. Place each glass on a FLAT with a DISH PAPER or on a side plate with a doily.

Uses

Cold, single hors-d'oeuvres.

Cocktail de Crevettes Roses

PRAWN COCKTAIL

Portions: 4

Quantity		Ingredients	
	1	lettuce	washed and dried
200g	8oz	peeled prawns	
½ x	recipe	Sauce Marie Rose (see page 28)	
	4	unshelled prawns	peel the shell from the body only
	1tsp	mock black caviar	
	1	lemon	cut into wedges
	¼	cucumber	grooves cut along it with a CANELLE KNIFE and sliced

Method

1 Finely CHIFFONADE the lettuce and arrange in the bottom of 4 shallow glass dishes or wide champagne glasses.
2 Place the peeled prawns on top.
3 NAPPER with the Sauce Marie Rose.

Service

Garnish each dish with a part-peeled prawn and a little of the mock caviar in the centre and the lemon wedges and cucumber slices on the sides. Place each dish on a FLAT with a DISH PAPER or on a side plate with a doily.

Uses

Cold, single hors-d'oeuvres.

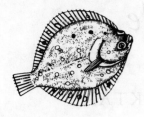

Cocktail de Fruits de Mer

SEAFOOD COCKTAIL

Portions: 4

Quantity		Ingredients	Preparation
	1	lettuce	washed and dried
50g	2oz	peeled prawns	
50g	2oz	scampi	poached
50g	2oz	mussels	cooked and de-bearded
50g	2oz	scallops	cooked
½ x	recipe	Sauce Marie Rose (see page 28)	
	¼	cucumber	grooves cut along it with a CANELLE KNIFE and sliced
	1	lemon	grooves cut along it with a CANELLE KNIFE and cut into wedges, pith from centre removed
	1	egg	hard-boiled and sieved
	1tsp	crab coral	sieved

Method

1 Finely CHIFFONADE the lettuce and arrange in the bottom of 4 shallow glass dishes or wide champagne glasses.
2 Cut the cooked and prepared prawns and scampi into a SALPICON.
3 Place the mussels and scallops on top.
4 NAPPER with the Sauce Marie Rose.

Service

Garnish each dish with the cucumber slices, lemon wedges, sieved egg and coral, then place each dish on a FLAT with DISH PAPER or on a side plate with a doily.

Uses

Cold, single hors-d'oeuvres.

Cocktail de Homard

LOBSTER COCKTAIL

Portions: 4

Quantity		Ingredients	
	1	lettuce	washed and dried
200g	8oz	lobster	
½ x	recipe	Sauce Marie Rose (see page 28)	
	4	tomatoes	made into TOMATO ROSES
	1	lemon	grooves cut along it with a CANELLE KNIFE and cut into wedges, pith from centre removed
	¼	cucumber	grooves cut along it with a CANELLE KNIFE and sliced

Method

1 Finely CHIFFONADE the lettuce and arrange in the bottom of 4 shallow glass dishes or wide champagne glasses.
2 Cut 4 slices from the lobster and reserve.
3 Cut the remaining lobster into a SALPICON.
4 Place the SALPICON of lobster on top of the lettuce.
5 NAPPER with the Sauce Marie Rose.

Service

Garnish each dish with a slice of lobster, a tomato rose, lemon wedges and cucumber slices, then place each dish on a FLAT with DISH PAPER or on a side plate with a doily.

Uses

Cold, single hors-d'oeuvres.

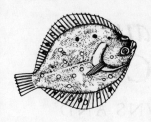

Cocktail de Poisson

FISH COCKTAIL

Portions: 4

Quantity		Ingredients	Preparation
	1	lettuce	washed and dried
200g	8oz	fish *or* shellfish	
½ x	recipe	Sauce Marie Rose (see page 28)	
Optional garnishes			
		crab *or* lobster coral	
		mock caviar, black *or* red	
		sieved hard-boiled egg	
		paprika	
		chopped parsley	
		TOMATO ROSES	

Method

1 Finely CHIFFONADE the lettuce and arrange in the bottom of 4 shallow glass dishes or wide champagne glasses.
2 Place the fish or shellfish on top of the lettuce.
3 NAPPER with the Sauce Marie Rose.

Service

Garnish each dish with one or more of the optional garnishes, then place each dish on a FLAT with a DISH PAPER or on a side plate with a doily.

Uses

Cold, single hors-d'oeuvres.

Crevettes au Beurre et Crème

POTTED PRAWNS AND CREAM

Portions: 4

Quantity		Ingredients	Preparation
200g	8oz	peeled prawns	
	pinch	salt	
	pinch	cayenne pepper	
	pinch	nutmeg	
200g	8oz	butter	melted
125ml	5fl oz	double cream	
	2	lemons	1 juiced; 1 peeled and sliced
	few sprigs	fresh parsley	washed

Method

1 Season the prawns to taste with the salt, cayenne pepper and nutmeg.
2 Divide between 4 ramekins.
3 Cream together the butter, cream and lemon juice.
4 Spread the cream mixture over the prawns in the ramekins and smooth the top level.
5 Chill until the mixture has set (about an hour).
6 Make a cut in each of the lemon slices from the centre out and twist the cut edges in opposite directions.

Service

Garnish each ramekin with a lemon twist and a little parsley. Serve in a water-lily serviette.

Uses

Cold, single hors-d'oeuvres.

Variation

As above but replace the double cream with 125ml (5fl oz) white wine and boiling the butter, wine, seasonings and prawns together in a pan before spooning into the ramekins.

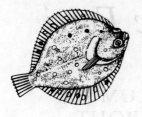

Crevettes avec Sauce Aïoli

PRAWNS WITH GARLIC MAYONNAISE

Portions: 4

Quantity		Ingredients
250g	10oz	unshelled prawns
½ x	recipe	Sauce Aïoli (see page 23)
10g	½oz	black mock caviar

Method

1 Peel the shell from the body only, leaving the head attached.
2 Make the Sauce Aïoli as given in the recipe and then spoon it into a piping bag.

Service

Place the prawns around the edge of a RAVIER dish, pipe rosettes of the Sauce Aïoli in the middle and garnish with the mock caviar.

Uses

Hors-d'oeuvre varié.

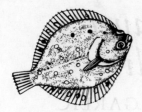

Concombre Farci Pêcheur

SLICES OF CUCUMBER FILLED WITH TROUT MOUSSE

Portions: 4

Quantity		Ingredients	Preparation
200g	8oz	trout fillets	
	½tsp	lemon juice	
		salt and pepper	
	1	egg	separated
	4tbsp	double cream	
	1-2 tsp	tomato purée	
	1	cucumber	
Sauce			
	2tbsp	shallots	finely chopped
	3	tomatoes	finely chopped
	1 sprig	fennel	
125ml	5fl oz	white wine	
200ml	8fl oz	vegetable stock	
125ml	¼ pint	double cream	
Garnish			
	1tsp	tomato CONCASSER	
	4 sprigs	dill	

Method

1 Process the trout in a food processor or blender until smooth.

2 Add the lemon juice, egg yolk, season and mix until smooth.

3 Add the egg white, cream and tomato purée and mix until smooth.

4 Chill for 1 hour.

5 Meanwhile, cut the cucumber into thirds, cut grooves along the sides using a CANELLE KNIFE and remove the seeds and flesh to leave a ring 7mm (¼ inch) thick. Leave to dry a little on paper kitchen towels.

6 Place the cucumber on tin foil – flesh side upwards – and fill with the trout mousse, then wrap the foil round the cucumber, securing the seams well.

7 Place the foil parcels in a saucepan, cover with water and simmer for 30 minutes.

8 Remove them from the pan, open, drain off any moisture, leave to cool, then chill them for 30 minutes.

9 Meanwhile make the sauce. Boil the shallots, tomatoes and fennel in the wine and stock until it has reduced to 125ml (¼ pint).

10 Remove the fennel, then liquidise the sauce in a food processor or blender until smooth and sieve it into a clean pan.

11 Stir in the cream and simmer gently until slightly thickened.

12 Season, leave to cool, then chill.

Service

Cut each cucumber into 4 slices and NAPPER 4 serving plates with the sauce. Place 3 slices of the stuffed cucumber in the centre of each plate. Garnish the cucumbers with a dot of the tomato CONCASSER and a sprig of dill.

Uses

_____

_____

_____

Variations

As above but replace the trout with any suitable fish, such as salmon.

Derivatives

_____

_____

_____

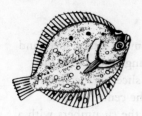

Coquilles Saint Jacques Mariné
MARINATED SCALLOPS

Portions: 4

Quantity	Ingredients
8	scallops with corals
4	limes
1	red pepper
1	green pepper
1	yellow pepper
1	red onion
6tbsp	olive oil
8	peppercorns
	salt
25g 1oz	coriander leaves

Method

1 Slice the scallops in half horizontally.
2 Cut 4 slices from 1 of the limes and squeeze the juice from the rest.
3 Slice the peppers and onion thinly.
4 Mix the oil, peppercorns, salt and coriander with the lime juice.
5 Add the scallops, peppers and onion.
6 Marinate overnight.

Service

Serve cold, garnished with the lime slices.

Uses

Variations

Derivatives

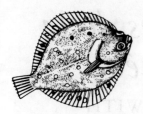

Crabe Dresse

DRESSED CRAB

Portions: 1

Quantity		Ingredients	Preparation
400–			
800g	1–1½lb	crab	cooked
125ml	¼ pint	vinaigrette	
	1tsp	Worcestershire sauce	
		salt and pepper	
200g	8oz	white breadcrumbs	sieved
125ml	¼ pint	double cream	
	1tbsp	oil	
Garnish			
	1	egg	hard-boiled and sieved
	1tsp	parsley	finely chopped

Method

1 Wash and scrub the crab well.
2 Remove the claws and legs.
3 Crack the claws, remove all the white meat and put it into a bowl.
4 Remove the undershell.
5 Remove all the white and brown meats and keep them in separate bowls.
6 Moisten the brown meat with the vinaigrette and the Worcestershire sauce.
7 Shred the white meat and season.
8 Soak the breadcrumbs in the cream.
9 Measure out an amount of the breadcrumb and cream mixture equal to half the volume of the brown crab meat.
10 Sieve the brown meat and mix it with the measured breadcrumbs and cream mixture and season.
11 Press out the edges of the shell, scrub it clean, dry it and brush it with the oil.

Service

Fill the shell with two thirds of the white meat, placing half of it at each end. Put the brown meat down the middle. Garnish with lines of the sieved egg and the parsley. Arrange the legs in a circle on a serving plate lined with DISH PAPER and rest the filled shell on the legs, which keep it from rocking.

Uses

Table d'hôte single hors-d'oeuvre.

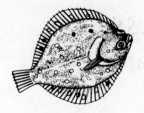

Demoiselles de la Méditerranée

KING PRAWNS WITH GARLIC MAYONNAISE

Portions: 4

Quantity	Ingredients	Preparation
12	unshelled king prawns	
1tbsp	oil	
½ x recipe	Sauce Aïoli (see page 23)	made thick
1tsp	black mock caviar	
1tsp	red mock caviar	
1 bunch	watercress	washed, dried and trimmed

Method

1 Lightly brush the king prawns with the oil so that they shine.
2 Make the Sauce Aïoli as given in the recipe, then spoon it into a piping bag with a star nozzle.

Service

Place 3 king prawns on each serving plate, overlapping them slightly. Pipe 2 rosettes of Sauce Aïoli next to them and garnish one with the red caviar and one with the black and decorate with the watercress.

Uses

Cold, single hors-d'oeuvres.

Émincé de Saumon Fumé

PARCELS OF SMOKED SALMON WITH YOGURT CREAM SAUCE

Portions: 4

Quantity		Ingredients	Preparation
Mousse			
75g	3oz	smoked salmon	
25g	1oz	smoked trout	
125ml	5fl oz	double cream	
Sauce			
125ml	5fl oz	double cream	
125ml	5fl oz	yogurt	
	1	lemon	juiced
		sugar to taste	
		salt and pepper	
	8 slices	smoked salmon	
Garnish			
100g	4oz	tomato CONCASSER	
25g	1oz sprigs	fresh dill	

Method

1 First, make the mousse. Process the smoked salmon and trout in a food processor or blender until smooth.
2 Place the purée in a bowl over ice and gradually beat in the cream.
3 Next, make the sauce. Mix together the cream, yogurt and lemon juice and add sugar and seasoning to taste.
4 Next, make up the parcels. Lay the smoked salmon slices out flat and put an eighth of the mousse in the centre. Fold the sides in to make small, square parcels.

NAPPER 4 plates with the sauce. Place 2 parcels in the centre of each plate, setting them at slight angles to one another. Garnish with small BOUQUETS of tomato CONCASSER and sprigs of dill.

Uses

_____

_____

_____

Variations

As above, but fill the parcels with any suitable mousse, e.g., prawn, smoked eel, mackerel, or lobster. As above but glaze the parcels with fish aspic and decorate with strips of blanched leek folded to look like the parcel has been tied with string.

Derivatives

_____

_____

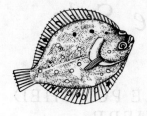

Farce de Poisson

FISH PASTE

Portions: 4

Quantity		Ingredients
400g	1lb	fish (whiting, pike, salmon, etc.)
50g	2oz	Panada (see page 7)
50g	2oz	egg white
500ml	1 pint	double cream
		Le Sel d'Épice (see page 5)
		salt and pepper

Method

1 Mince the fish twice through the fine plate on a mincer.
2 Add the Panada and egg white and mix well together.
3 Pass through a fine sieve.
4 Beat it well in a bowl over ice.
5 Gradually add the cream, beating it well over the ice.
6 Season to taste.

Service

As required.

Uses

Form into quennelles, use as a stuffing or in terrines.

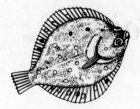

Goujons de Sole Orientale

STICKS OF SOLE POACHED IN WINE AND HERB SAUCE

Portions: 4

Quantity		Ingredients	Preparation
125ml	¼ pint	white wine	
125ml	¼ pint	fish stock	
25ml	1fl oz	olive oil	
200g	8oz	tomatoes	made into a CONCASSER
	¼tsp	saffron	
	1	bay leaf	
	¼tsp	fennel seeds	
	¼tsp	coriander seeds	
	¼tsp	peppercorns	
	1 clove	garlic	crushed
400g	1lb	lemon sole	skinned and cut into goujons
Garnish			
	1	lemon	sliced and pith removed
25g	1oz	dill	pick the crowns from the stems and reserve

Method

1 Place the wine, fish stock, oil, tomato CONCASSER, herbs and spices and garlic in a pan.
2 Bring to the boil and check the seasoning.
3 Add the goujons of sole and poach gently until cooked
4 Leave to cool in the sauce.

Service

Serve neatly in a white, oval SUR LE PLAT DISH and garnish with the lemon slices and crowns of dill.
Serve on a FLAT with DISH PAPER and serviette gondalas.

Uses	Variations
Hors-d'oeuvre varié and single fish hors-d'oeuvres.	As above but use trout DARNES instead of lemon sole for Truite Darne à l'Orientale.

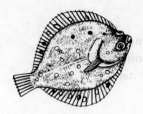

Harengs à la Portugaise

PORTUGUESE-STYLE HERRINGS

Portions: 4

Quantity		Ingredients	
200g	½lb	onions	finely chopped
100g	4oz	celery	washed and cut into short, thickish julienne
	1 clove	garlic	finely chopped
125ml	¼ pint	oil	
400g	1lb	tomatoes	made into a CONCASSER
100–			
125g	4–5oz	tomato purée	
	1 sprig	thyme	
		salt and pepper	
	1	bay leaf	
125ml	¼ pint	white wine	
	4	herrings	

Method

1 Sweat the onions, celery and garlic in the oil until cooked.
2 Add the tomato CONCASSER and cook until soft.
3 Add the tomato purée, which gives it a wonderful colour.
4 Add the seasoning herbs and wine.
5 Clean and prepare the herrings whole and CISLER or cut into DARNES.
6 Place the herrings in a dish, cover with the sauce, cover with a paper lid and poach until cooked. Then leave to cool until cold.

Service

Spoon the herrings into a white SUR LE PLAT DISH and NAPPER with sauce. Garnish as required.

Uses

Hors-d'oeuvre varié and table d'hôte single hors-d'oeuvres.

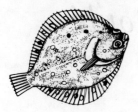

Harengs Dieppoise
SOUSED HERRINGS

Portions: 4

Quantity		Ingredients	Preparation
	4	herrings	scaled, filleted and trimmed
		salt and pepper	
25g	1oz	carrot	peeled, grooved with CANELLE KNIFE and thinly sliced
25g	1oz	pickling onions	peeled and sliced into thin rings
	½	bay leaf	
	1 sprig	thyme	
	6	peppercorns	
	1	parsley stalk	
125ml	5fl oz	vinegar	
125ml	5fl oz	water	
	1 sprig	parsley	washed

Method

1 Wash the herrings well, season them, then roll them up and secure the ends with cocktail sticks.
2 Place in an earthenware dish.
3 Blanch the carrots and onions for 2–3 minutes, then sprinkle them over the fish.
4 Mix the remaining ingredients together and pour over the fish.
5 Cover with an oiled sheet of greaseproof paper and cook in a moderate (350°F/180°C/Gas Mark 4) oven for 15–20 minutes.
6 Leave to cool until cold.

Service

Serve in a white SUR LE PLAT DISH, garnished with the onions and carrots, moistened with the cooking liquor and decorated with the parsley.

Uses

Table d'hôte hors-d'oeuvres and hors-d'oeuvre varié.

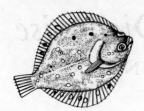

Harengs Roulé

ROLLMOPS

Portions: 4

Quantity		Ingredients	Preparation
	4	herrings	washed, trimmed, backbone removed
50g	2oz	sea salt	
25g *or*	1oz *or*		
10g	½oz	onions *or* gherkins	peeled and shredded *or* quartered
Pickling liquor			
100g	4oz	onions	peeled and shredded
1l	2 pints	white wine vinegar	
500ml	1 pint	white wine	
250ml	½ pint	white vinegar	
	4	bay leaves	
	20	dried chillies	
	40	peppercorns	
	40	allspice berries	
	40	coriander seeds	
50g	2oz	brown sugar	
Garnish			
	1	lettuce	washed and dried
	1	lemon	grooves cut along it with a CANELLE KNIFE and sliced
	4	gherkins	cut into fans

Method

1 Sprinkle the herrings with the sea salt and leave overnight.
2 Wash under running water for 1 hour (to remove the salt), then pat dry with kitchen paper.

3 Place the onions or gherkins on the herrings and roll them up from head to tail, secure each closed with a cocktail stick and place in a deep tray.

4 Place the pickling liquor ingredients in a pan, bring to the boil, simmer for 5 minutes then leave to cool until cold.
5 Pour the liquor over the herrings.
6 Marinate for 7–10 days before using.

Service

Remove the rollmops from the marinade and drain. Remove the cocktail sticks, place the rollmops neatly in a white SUR LE PLAT DISH on a bed of lettuce, then decorate with the lemon slices and gherkin fans.

Uses

Table d'hôte hors-d'oeuvres, hors-d'oeuvre varié and canapés.

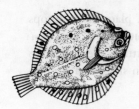

Hure de Saumon aux Poivre Vert avec Sauce Citron

TERRINE OF SALMON WITH GREEN PEPPERCORNS AND TOMATO, HERB AND LEMON SAUCE

Portions: 2

Quantity		Ingredients	Preparation
1½kg	3lb	salmon	
500ml	1 pint	white wine	
50g	2oz	parsley, chervil, tarragon	
	10	lemons	peeled
750ml	1½ pints	aspic (see page 4)	
Filling			
	8	hard-boiled eggs	chopped
200g	8oz	pimento	finely diced
50g	2oz	green peppercorns	
50g	2oz	shallots	chopped
Garnish			
1 x	recipe	Sauce Citron (see page 25)	
50g	2oz	watercress	washed and dried
50g	2oz	tomato CONCASSER	
10g	½oz sprigs	dill	

Method

1 Cut the salmon into strips.
2 Marinate in the wine and herbs for 1 hour.
3 Poach in the marinade for 2 minutes until cooked.
4 Cut the lemons into dice.

5 Layer the salmon, aspic and
   fillings in a terrine in the
   following order: aspic, fish,
   filling, fish, filling, aspic – leaving
   each layer to set before adding the
   next, then chill for 2 hours.

Service

NAPPER the serving plate with the
Sauce Citron, coating it. Turn the
terrine out and slice it into 1.5-cm
(½-inch) thick slices, place them
centrally on the plate and garnish
with the watercress, tomato
CONCASSER and sprigs of dill.

Uses

_____

_____

_____

Variations

Set in individual moulds.

Derivatives

_____

_____

_____

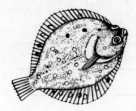

Le Chapeau d'Isa

TWO-COLOURED TROUT MOUSSE

Portions: 8–10

Quantity		Ingredients	Preparation
150g	6oz	smoked trout fillets	
100ml	3½fl oz	white wine sauce	
	3tbsp	fish stock	
	4 leaves	gelatine	soaked in cold water
100ml	3½fl oz	double cream	lightly whipped
		salt and pepper	
	2tbsp	spinach purée	
	pinch	saffron	
		oil	
Garnish			
10g	½oz	salmon roe	
10g	½oz	rose petals	
10g	½ oz	chive flowers	

Method

1 Purée the trout fillets and white wine sauce together in a food processor or blender, then pass the mixture through a fine sieve to remove any lumps.

2 Heat the fish stock, add the soaked gelatine and stir until dissolved.

3 Add the mixture to the smoked trout purée.

4 When mixture has almost set, whisk in a quarter of the cream, then fold in the rest.

5 Season to taste.

6 Divide the trout mixture between 2 bowls and add the spinach purée to one and the saffron to the other, mixing each half of mixture thoroughly, then spoon each into separate piping bags.

7 Oil 8–10 tiny DARIOLE moulds and pipe alternate lines of green and yellow trout mousse into them.

8 Chill until set (about an hour).

Service

Dip the moulds into hot water for a few seconds and turn them out onto separate plates. Garnish each with salmon roe, a rose petal and a chive flower.

Uses

_____

_____

_____

Variations

_____

_____

_____

Derivatives

_____

_____

_____

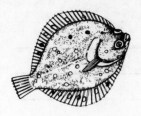

Mayonnaise de Fruits de Mer

SEAFOOD MAYONNAISE

Portions: 4

Quantity		Ingredients	Preparation
50g	2oz	peeled prawns	
50g	2oz	scampi	
50g	2oz	scallops	
50g	2oz	mussels	
50g	2oz	white fish	
250ml	½ pint	mayonnaise	
	1	lettuce	washed and dried
		salt and pepper	
Garnish			
5g	¼oz	black mock caviar	
	4	unshelled prawns	peel the shell from the body only

Method

1 Cook the shellfish and fish.
2 Flake or cut into a SALPICON.
3 Season to taste.
4 Mix in half the mayonnaise.
5 CHIFFONADE the lettuce.
6 Season the rest of the mayonnaise and adjust to a coating consistency, adding ½ teaspoon of boiling water.

Service

Place the chiffonade of lettuce in a RAVIER dish or on a FLAT and put the shellfish and fish mixture on top *or* mould the mixture into quennelles using two wetted dessertspoons and coat with the thinned mayonnaise. Garnish with the caviar and part-peeled prawns.

Uses

Table d'hôte hors-d'oeuvres and hors-d'oeuvre varié.

Variations

As above but all fish *or* shellfish instead of mixture and, if serving all together on one RAVIER OR FLAT, place the mixture on the lettuce in the shape of a fish, coat with the thinned mayonnaise and use half slices of cucumber to create a scale pattern and strips of anchovy to delineate the gills, eye and tail for Mayonnaise avec Poisson.

As above but use 200g (8oz) salmon instead of the shellfish and fish (cook it in *court bouillon*, see page 2, and flake when cold) and serve as the Mayonnaise avec Poisson for Mayonnaise avec Saumon.

Mousse de Crevettes Roses

PRAWN MOUSSE

Portions: 4

Quantity		Ingredients	Preparation
500ml	1 pint	aspic (see page 4)	
125ml	¼ pint	velouté	
100g	4oz	peeled prawns	sieved
	6 leaves	gelatine	soaked in cold water
		salt and pepper	
125ml	¼ pint	double cream	lightly whipped
Garnish			
	16	unshelled prawns	peel the shell from the body only

Method

1 Line 4 ramekins with half the aspic and leave to set for about an hour.
2 Pour the rest of the aspic in a thin layer on a FLAT plate and leave to set, then cut into diamonds.
3 Heat the velouté and add the sieved prawns.
4 Drain the gelatine, then add it to the velouté mixture, stirring until it melts.
5 Season, then leave it to cool and begin to set over ice.
6 Fold in the lightly whipped cream.
7 Pour the mousse into the moulds and level the tops. Chill until set (about an hour).

Service

Dip the moulds briefly into hot water, then carefully turn the mousses out onto a MIRRORED FLAT. Decorate around them with the aspic diamonds and garnish with the semi-peeled prawns.

Uses

Single, cold hors-d'oeuvres.

Variation

As above but use salmon instead of peeled prawns for Mousse de Saumon.

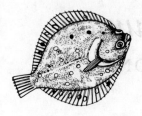

Pâté de Poisson Fumé

SMOKED FISH PÂTÉ

Portions: 8–10

Quantity		Ingredients	Preparation
400g	1lb	smoked fish	
300g	12oz	butter	softened
125ml	¼ pint	white wine	
or	1	lemon	juiced
140ml	7fl oz	double cream	
		salt and pepper	
Garnish			
	1	lemon	peeled and sliced
	8–10 sprigs	parsley	washed

Method

1 Flake the fish, removing any skin or bone.
2 Mix with half the butter and all the lemon juice *or* white wine.
3 Season to taste.
4 Pass the mixture through a fine sieve.
5 Beat in the cream.
6 Either spoon the mixture into 8–10 ramekins *or* a terrine and smooth the top level.
7 Cover with the remaining butter to seal.
8 Cut each slice of lemon from the centre out and turn the cut edges away from each other to form twists.

Service

Garnish the ramekins *or* terrine with the lemon twists and parsley, then serve on a water-lily serviette.

Uses

Cold, single hors-d'oeuvres.

Variations

As above but use smoked mackerel instead of the smoked fish for Pâté de Maquereau Fumé.
As above but use smoked salmon instead of the smoked fish for Pâté de Saumon Fumé.
As above but use smoked trout instead of the smoked fish for Pâté de Truite Fumé.

Pâté de Saumon

POTTED SALMON

Portions: 6

Quantity	Ingredients	Preparation
200g 8oz	fillet of salmon	
2 blades	mace	
1 pinch	ground gloves	
½	small bay leaf	
6	peppercorns	crushed
	salt	
150g 6oz	butter	
75g 3oz	clarified butter	melted
Garnish		
2	lemons	peeled and divided into segments
25g 1oz	black mock caviar	
6 slices	bread	toasted and cut into fingers

Method

1 Place the salmon in an ovenproof dish with the spices and seasoning.
2 Cover with the butter and cover with a lid.
3 Bake the salmon in a moderate (350°F/180°C/Gas Mark 4) oven for 15–25 minutes until it is just cooked.
4 Drain the fish, straining the cooking liquor and reserving it.
5 Skim the butter from the cooking liquor.
6 Process the fish with the skimmed off butter in a food processor or blender until smooth.

7 Spoon the fish mixture into PARISIENNE GOBLETS, and leave to cool. When cold, cover with a thin layer of the melted clarified butter.
8 Chill for at least 24 hours.

Service

Decorate the top with the lemon segments, arranging them in a flower pattern. Place the black mock caviar in the centre. Serve with hot fingers of toast.

Variations

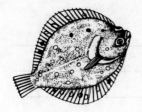

Rouget Niçoise

RED MULLET WITH TOMATO AND PEPPERS SAUCE

Portions: 4

Quantity		Ingredients	Preparation
400g	1lb	onions	finely chopped
	1 clove	garlic	finely chopped
125ml	¼ pint	oil	
400g	1lb	tomatoes	made into a CONCASSER
100/125g	4–5oz	tomato purée	
	1 sprig	thyme	
	1	bay leaf	
		salt and pepper	
125ml	¼ pint	white stock	
	1	red pepper	blanched, skinned and cut into julienne
	1	green pepper	blanched, skinned and cut into julienne
10g	½oz	black olives	stoned
5g	½oz	parsley	finely chopped
4 x 100g	4 x 4oz	red mullets	washed, scaled and trimmed

Method

1 Sweat the onions and garlic in the oil until cooked.
2 Add the tomato CONCASSER and cook until soft.
3 Add the tomato purée, which gives it a wonderful colour.
4 Add the herbs, seasoning and stock.
5 Reserving some to garnish the dish later, add the julienne of red and green peppers and stoned black olives.
6 Poach the red mullet in the sauce, covered with a greaseproof paper lid and the lid, in a 400°F/200°C (Gas Mark 6) oven for 10 minutes until just cooked. Then leave to cool until cold.

Service

Place the fishes on a white SUR LE PLAT DISH and NAPPER with the poaching sauce. Garnish with the reserved julienne of red and green peppers, olives and parsley.

Uses

Table d'hôte hors-d'oeuvres.

Variation

As above but use mackerel steaks instead of the red mullet for Suprême de Maquereau Niçoise.

Roulades de Saumon Fumé et Fruits de Mer

SMOKED SALMON AND SEAFOOD ROLLS

Portions: 4

Quantity		Ingredients	Preparation
50g	2oz	peeled prawns	cut SALPICON
50g	2oz	scallops	cooked and cut SALPICON
50g	2oz	scampi	cooked and cut SCALPICON
50g	2oz	white crab meat	flaked
		salt and pepper	
250ml	½ pint	mayonnaise	
200g	8oz	smoked salmon	sliced
	¼	cucumber	grooves cut along it with a CANELLE KNIFE, thinly sliced and formed into cornets
5g	¼oz	black mock caviar	
5g	¼oz	red mock caviar	
	1	lettuce	washed and dried
	1	lemon	cut into wedges
	1tbsp	oil	

Method

1 Mix the prepared seafood together in a bowl and season.
2 Mix in the mayonnaise.
3 Place the seafood mayonnaise on the smoked salmon slices.
4 Roll the salmon into cylinders and carefully trim the ends.
5 Fill the cucumber cornets with the red and black caviar.

Service

Serve the roulades on a bed of lettuce, brushed lightly with the oil, garnished with the cucumber cornets and lemon wedges.

Uses

Cold, single hors-d'oeuvres.

Variations

As above but replace the seafood with 100g (4oz) peeled prawns, the mayonnaise with the same amount of sauce Marie Rose (see page 28) and garnish with cucumber and lines of black mock caviar between each roulade for Roulades de Saumon Fumé et Crevettes Roses.

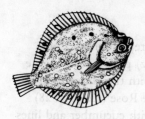

Salade Buissonière aux Poissons Fumé

SMOKED FISH SALAD

Portions: 8

Quantity		Ingredients	Preparation
	1 clove	garlic	
500ml	1 pint	olive oil	
	18	black peppercorns	
100g	4oz	green peppercorns	
200g	8oz	smoked salmon	
400g	1lb	smoked trout	
400g	1lb	smoked eel	
200g	8oz	smoked oysters	
200g	8oz	carrots	cut into julienne
200g	8oz	celeriac	cut into julienne
	1	oak leaf lettuce	washed and trimmed
	1	curly endive	washed and trimmed
	1 bunch	watercress	washed and trimmed
25g	1oz	shallots	finely chopped
25g	1oz	chervil	finely chopped
25g	1oz	parsley	finely chopped
25g	1oz	fresh ginger	peeled and cut into julienne

Method

1 Boil the garlic, olive oil, green and black peppercorns and carrot and celeriac, for 5 minutes, then leave to cool.

2 Slice the smoked fish and oysters very thinly.

3 Brush with the flavoured oil.

4 Mix all the salad ingredients and herbs together, except the ginger.

Service

Arrange the salad in the centre of
the serving plate leaving a margin
around the edge. Place the smoked
fish around the outside. Finish the
salad with the julienne of ginger.

Uses

_____

_____

_____

Variations

Alternative salads for centre that are
suitable.

Derivatives

_____

_____

_____

_____

Fish and Seafood Hors-d'Oeuvres 195

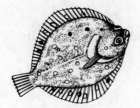

Salade de Crabe Porgenteuil

SALAD OF CRAB AND ASPARAGUS WITH A CHIVE VINAIGRETTE

Portions: 8

Quantity		Ingredients	Preparation
1½kg	3lb	asparagus spears	trimmed
200g	8oz	mixed salad leaves	washed, dried and trimmed
500ml	1 pint	white wine vinegar	
500ml	1 pint	olive oil	
		salt and pepper	
1kg	2lb	white crab meat	
	1	lime	juiced
	pinch	cayenne pepper	
	1 bunch	chives	chopped

Method

1 Cook the asparagus spears in boiling water until *al dente* and refresh. Drain well.
2 Dress the salad leaves with the vinegar, olive oil and salt and pepper.
3 Mix the crab meat with the lime juice and cayenne pepper.

Service

Arrange equal amounts of the salad in the middle of 8 plates. Spoon some crab meat neatly onto the centre of the salad and garnish with the asparagus and chives.

Uses

Variations

Derivatives

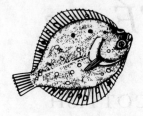

Sardine à l'Huile
SARDINES

Portions: 4

Quantity	Ingredients	Preparation
1	lemon	
1 tin	sardines	drained
5g ¼oz	parsley	washed

Method

1 Cut the lemon into wedges, trim them, then slice them into triangles.

Service

Place the sardines in a RAVIER dish and garnish with lemon triangles and parsley.

Uses

Hors-d'oeuvre varié.

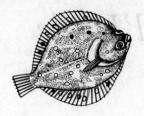

Saumon d'Écosse Mariné

MARINATED SCOTTISH SALMON

Portions: 2

Quantity		Ingredients	Preparation
1½kg	3–3½lb	whole Scottish salmon	
30g	1¼oz	salt	
15g	¾oz	sugar	
25g	1oz	fresh dill	
	1tbsp	white peppercorns	crushed
Garnish			
250ml	½ pint	double cream	lightly whipped
	6	lemons	cut into wedges
50g	2oz	black mock caviar	
50g	2oz sprigs	dill	
	½	cucumber	thinly sliced, slices halved
200g	8oz	curly endive	washed and trimmed

Method

1 Fillet the salmon, removing the bones, and put in a large enough dish for it to lay flat.
2 Mix the remaining ingredients together, spread over the salmon, cover and chill.
3 Marinate the fish for 24 hours, occasionally moistening it with the liquid that is produced.
4 Wash the fish in cold water and cut the flesh into fine julienne.

Service

Stand the julienne of salmon in a 5-cm (2-inch) pastry cutter on each plate. Spoon a little of the cream on top and smooth with a palette knife. Remove the cutter and decorate with the mock caviar, a lemon wedge and a small sprig of dill. Place the half slices of cucumber around the foot of the salmon julienne, overlapping them and finish with the curly endive.

Uses

Derivatives

Variations

As above but to serve 4: use 350g (14oz) of salmon, thinly sliced and, for the marinade, use the juice of 2 limes and a tablespoon each of chopped chives, chervil and tarragon and meaux mustard (marinate for just 10 minutes) served on a plate garnished with lemon halves.

Saumon Fumé d'Ecosse

SCOTTISH SMOKED SALMON

Portions: 4–10

Quantity		Ingredients	Preparation
Side			
1½kg	3lb	side of smoked Scottish salmon	
	5	lemons	
Plated			
200g	8oz	smoked Scottish salmon	
	2	lemons	
	¼	cucumber	grooves cut along it with a CANELLE KNIFE and sliced

Method

1 For the side-dish version, trim the side of smoked salmon and remove any bones.
2 Very lightly, brush it with oil.
3 Place the salmon on a wooden salmon board.
4 For the plated version, slice the smoked salmon thinly.
5 Cut the lemons in half through the equator on the angle. Trim the peel from the edge on the angle. Tie and loop. *Or,* cut the lemons in half and tie them in a muslin bag.

Service

Garnish with the lemon and cucumber.

Uses

Cold, single hors-d'oeuvres.

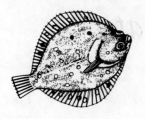

Suprême de Maquereau Fumé

SMOKED MACKEREL SUPREMES

Portions: 4

Quantity	Ingredients	Preparation
4	smoked mackerel fillets	
1 tbsp	oil	
Garnish		
1	lettuce	washed and dried
1	lemon	cut into wedges
1 sprig	parsley	washed

Method

1 Skin and trim the mackerel fillets.
2 Cut them into SUPREMES (4 per small fillet; 5 per large fillet).
3 Lightly brush with the oil.

Service

Serve the mackerel SUPREMES on a bed of the lettuce. Garnish with the lemon wedges and parsley. Serve with a suitable sauce.

Uses

Table d'hôte single hors-d'oeuvres.

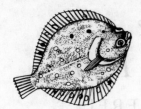

Taramasalata

Portions: 10–12

Quantity		Ingredients	Preparation
100g	4oz	white breadcrumbs	sieved
500ml	1 pint	milk	
1½kg	3lb	smoked cod roe	
	3 cloves	garlic	crushed
25g	1oz	tomato purée	
125ml	¼ pint	olive oil	
	1	lemon	juiced
		salt and pepper	
Garnish			
5g	¼oz	parsley	washed
10g	½oz	black olives	stoned

Method

1 Mix the breadcrumbs with the milk then lift them out and squeeze out the milk.
2 Place the soaked bread and the cod roe in a food processor or blender and mix at high speed.
3 Add the garlic and tomato purée and mix in.
4 Slowly add the oil and lemon juice.
5 Adjust the seasoning to taste, if necessary.
6 Spoon the mixture into a small soufflé dish or 10–12 ramekins and chill until set.

Service

Garnish with the parsley and black olives and serve with a suitable salad.

Uses

Table d'hôte hors-d'oeuvres.

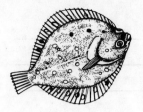

Terrine de Fruits de Mer

SEAFOOD TERRINE

Portions: 10–12

Quantity		Ingredients	Preparation
1kg	2lb	mussels	cooked and shelled
1kg	2lb	prawns	cooked and shelled
1kg	2lb	cockles	cooked and shelled
250ml	½ pint	white wine	
	1 sprig	dill	chopped
	1 sprig	chervil	chopped
	1 sprig	chives	chopped
25g	1oz	parsley	chopped
1kg	2lb	asparagus, tinned	drained
1½l	3 pints	fish aspic (see page 4)	
Garnish			
		salad leaves (as available)	washed and dried
		tomato CONCASSER	

Method

1 Marinate the seafood in the wine and herbs for 1 hour.
2 Place the seafood and asparagus in the terrine in layers: seafood, asparagus, seafood, asparagus.
3 Fill with the fish aspic to seal and chill until set.

Service

Dip the terrines in very hot water for a few seconds, then carefully unmould and cut the terrines into thickish slices. Arrange them neatly on individual plates and garnish with the salad leaves and tomato CONCASSER.

Uses

_____

_____

_____

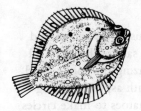

Terrine de Poisson

FISH TERRINE

Portions: 8–10

Quantity		Ingredients	Preparation
50g	20z	butter	melted
		salt and pepper	
1kg	2lb	lemon sole fillets	skinned and trimmed
1 x	recipe	Farce (whiting) (see page 173)	
400g	1lb	salmon fillet	skinned and trimmed
1 x	recipe	Farce (salmon) (see page 173)	
25g	10z	garnishing paste	finely diced
500ml	1 pint	aspic (see page 4)	
Garnish			
		salad leaves (as available)	washed and dried
		black grapes	blanched

Method

1 Butter and season a terrine.
2 Hammer a few lemon sole fillets out enough to line and overhang the terrine.
3 Trim the remaining fillets into batons.
4 Place a layer of the whiting Farce in the bottom of the terrine.
5 Cut the salmon fillet into batons and place in lines on the Farce.
6 Cover the batons with more whiting Farce.
7 Place a layer of salmon Farce in the terrine.
8 Place lines of sole batons over the Farce.
9 Cover with salmon Farce.
10 Continue in this way until the terrine has been filled with layers of Farce and batons.
11 When it is full, cover the top with the overhanging sole fillets.
12 Cover with a buttered paper lid and chill overnight to set it.
13 Cook it in a bain-marie and, when cooked, press by placing a 1kg (2lb) weight on top and leave to cool.
14 Unmould the terrine by dipping it first in hot water, then slice some portions and glaze with some of the aspic (portions and the rest of the terrine).
15 MIRROR A FLAT with some of the aspic and set the remaining aspic, cutting it into 'croûtons' when it has done so.

Service

Trim the glazed portions and terrine to neaten, then carefully transfer them to the mirrored FLAT and garnish as required.

Uses

Cold, single hors-d'oeuvres.

Variations

As above but use a savarin mould and 1kg (2lbs) salmon Farce to fill the mould, glazing the cooked and cooled item with aspic and using 400g (1lb) tomatoes to make circles, julienne and a coulis, and 4 sliced king prawns, to decorate it to look like a turban for Turbon de Poisson avec Coulis de Tomate (the tomato coulis being served in a sauce-boat).

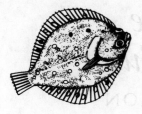

Terrine de Poisson
SEAFOOD TERRINE

Portions: 8–10

Quantity		Ingredients	Preparation
400g	1lb	peeled prawns	
400g	1lb	cockles	drained
800g	2lb	mussels	cooked and beards removed
	4	eggs	hardboiled and diced
500g	1¼lb	asparagus	drained and diced
400g	1lb	crab sticks	diced
1l	2 pints	fish aspic (see page 4)	

Method

1 Mix the prawns, cockles, mussels, egg, asparagus and crab sticks together.
2 Place in a clean terrine.
3 Melt the aspic and fill the terrine with it.
4 Chill until it has set.

Service

Dip the terrine briefly in hot water and unmould its contents carefully onto a FLAT with DISH PAPER and serviette gondalas. Serve with a suitable salad.

Uses

Cold, single hors-d'oeuvres.

Timbale de Saumon Fumé

SMOKED SALMON TERRINE

Portions: 12

Quantity		Ingredients	Preparation
500ml	1 pint	aspic (see page 4)	
1kg	2lb	smoked salmon trimmings	chopped
500ml	1 pint	mayonnaise	
500ml	1 pint	double cream	lightly whipped
5g	¼ pint	white wine	
5g	¼oz	gelatine	
	2	lemons	juiced
		salt and pepper	
Garnish			
	2	lemons	cut into wedges
200g	8oz	salad leaves	

Method

1 Line 12 small dariole moulds with aspic, leave to set, then decorate the bottom with a little of the smoked salmon.

2 In a food processor, mix the mayonnaise and the rest of the smoked salmon and season to taste.

3 Fold the cream into the mayonnaise and salmon mixture.

4 Gently heat the wine and dissolve the gelatine in it, then stir it into the mayonnaise, salmon and cream mixture, together with the lemon juice.

5 Pour the mixture into the moulds and chill until they have set (about an hour).

Service

Dip the moulds into hot water for a moment, then carefully turn the contents out onto individual serving plates and garnish with the lemon wedges and salad leaves.

Uses

_____

_____

_____

Variations

_____

_____

_____

Derivatives

_____

_____

_____

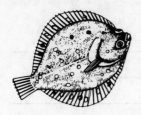

Tomates avec Crevettes

TOMATOES WITH PRAWNS

Portions: 4

Quantity	Ingredients	Preparation
2	beefsteak tomatoes	blanched and skinned
200g 8oz	peeled prawns	
½ x recipe	Sauce Marie Rose (see page 28)	
Garnish		
1	curly endive	washed and dried
8	unshelled prawns	peel the shell from the body only
½tsp	black mock caviar	

Method

1 Cut the tomatoes in half through the equator and remove the seeds.
2 Mix the peeled prawns with the sauce Marie Rose, then stuff the tomato halves with the mixture.

Service

Serve the tomatoes on a bed of curly endive, garnished with the part-peeled prawns and the mock caviar.

Uses

Single fish hors-d'oeuvres.

Truite Fumé avec Sauce Raifort

SMOKED TROUT WITH HORSERADISH SAUCE

Portions: 4

Quantity	Ingredients	Preparation
4	smoked trout oil	cooked and cleaned
1	lettuce	washed and dried
1	lemon	cut into wedges
1 sprig	parsley	washed
¼	cucumber	grooves cut along it with a CANELLE KNIFE and sliced
1 x recipe	Sauce Railfort (see page 31)	

Method

1 Either brush the trout with oil as it is or skin the body of the trout and then brush it lightly with oil.
2 Place the lemon wedges in squeezers, if available.

Uses

Cold, single hors-d'oeuvres.

Service

Place the trout on a bed of lettuce, put a little parsley in the eye and the cucumber slices on the tail. Place the lemon squeezer at the head and serve the Sauce Railfort separately in a sauce-boat.

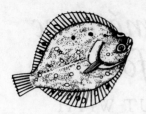

Truite Mariné

POACHED TROUT

Portions: 4

Quantity		Ingredients	Preparation
	4	trout	
250ml	½ pint	*court bouillon* (see page 2)	
125ml	¼ pint	white wine	
	1	lemon	peeled and sliced
	1tsp	tarragon leaves	washed

Method

1 Wash and remove the scales from the trout.
2 Trim off the fins and tail.
3 Clean again.
4 Poach in the *court bouillon* and white wine until just tender.
5 Leave to cool in the *court bouillon*.
6 Skin the body.

Service

Place the prepared trout on a FLAT and moisten a little with the cooking liquor. Decorate with the tarragon leaves and slices of lemon.

Uses

Cold, single hors-d'oeuvres.

7 COMPOUND SALADS

Coleslaw

Portions: 4

Quantity		Ingredients	Preparation
200g	8oz	crisp white cabbage	
50g	2oz	carrot	washed and peeled
50g	2oz	onion	
		salt and pepper	
125ml	5fl oz	mayonnaise	

Method

1 Trim the outer leaves from the cabbage, cut in half, remove the stalk and finely shred the rest, forming long, fine strips.
2 Grate the carrot.
3 Finely shred the onion.
4 Mix the cabbage, carrots and onions together and season.
5 Add the mayonnaise to the vegetables and mix together well.

Service

Spoon the salad neatly into a serving dish.

Uses

Buffets or as required.

Salade à l'Andalouse

ANDALUSIAN SALAD

Portions: 4

Quantity		Ingredients	Preparation
100g	4oz	long-grain rice	washed
25g	1oz	onions	finely chopped
5g	¼oz	parsley	finely chopped
125ml	¼ pint	vinaigrette	
	1 clove	garlic	finely chopped
		salt and pepper	
	2	green peppers	blanched, skinned and de-seeded
50g	2oz	tomatoes	blanched and skinned

Method

1 Cook the rice in boiling salted water until fluffy, then refresh.
2 Mix with chopped onions, parsley, vinaigrette (reserving about a tablespoon) and garlic and season to taste.
3 Cut the peppers into fine julienne.
4 Cut the tomatoes into wedges (4–6).

Service

Spoon the rice neatly into a white SUR LE PLAT DISH, doming it slightly. Place the tomatoes down one side and brush them with the reserved vinaigrette. Place the pepper down the other side and brush with vinaigrette.

Uses

Buffets.

Salade Allemande
GERMAN SALAD

Portions: 4

Quantity		Ingredients	Preparation
150g	6oz	potatoes	cooked and diced
150g	6oz	dessert apples	peeled and diced
100g	4oz	dill pickle	diced
100g	4oz	salt herrings	skinned and diced
125ml	¼ pint	mayonnaise	
		salt and pepper	
100g	4oz	beetroot	drained, diced and dried, reserving a few slices
Garnish			
	1	lettuce	washed and dried
	2	eggs	hard-boiled

Method

1 Mix the potatoes, apples, pickle and herring together with the mayonnaise.
2 Season to taste.
3 Add the beetroot just before serving.

Service

Place the salad on a bed of lettuce in a white SUR LE PLAT DISH. Garnish with the wedges of hard-boiled egg and the reserved slices of beetroot.

Uses

Table d'hôte hors-d'oeuvres.

Salade Bonne Femme

APPLE AND CELERY SALAD WITH SOUR CREAM

Portions: 4

Quantity		Ingredients	Preparation
200g	8oz	dessert apples	peel and cored
100g	4oz	celery	washed
	1	lemon	juiced
125ml	5fl oz	double cream	lightly whipped
		salt and pepper	

Method

1 Cut the apples into thickish short julienne.
2 Cut the celery into thickish short julienne.
3 Add the lemon juice to the cream and season to taste.
4 Mix the apples and celery with the sour cream.

Service

Spoon the salad neatly into a salad bowl.

Uses

Buffets or as required.

Salade Carmen

CHICKEN, RICE AND VEGETABLE SALAD

Portions: 4

Quantity		Ingredients	Preparation
200g	8oz	cooked white of chicken	skinned
50g	2oz	petits pois	cooked and refreshed
100g	4oz	long-grain rice	cooked and refreshed
	2	red peppers	de-seeded and trimmed
¼ x	recipe	French Mustard Dressing (see page 15)	
		salt and pepper	
Garnish			
	1	lettuce	washed and dried
	1tsp	tarragon	finely chopped

Method

1 Cut the chicken into fine dice.
2 Mix the chicken, petits pois and rice together.
3 Cut the peppers into fine dice and mix with rice and chicken.
4 Moisten with the vinaigrette and season to taste.

Uses

Buffets, table d'hôte hors-d'oeuvres or hors-d'oeuvre varié.

Service

Arrange a bed of lettuce on a white SUR LE PLAT DISH and spoon the salad into the middle of it, forming a loose dome.

Salade Columbia

COLUMBIAN SALAD

Portions: 4

Quantity		Ingredients	Preparation
600g	1½lb	dessert apples	peeled and cored
	1	lemon	juiced
	4	bananas	peeled
100g	4oz	black grapes	washed
	1 head	celery	trimmed, peeled and washed
250ml	½ pint	mayonnaise	
		salt and pepper	
Garnish			
	1	lettuce	washed and dried
25g	1oz	pistachio nuts	blanched, skinned and chopped

Method

1 Slice the apples and marinate in the lemon juice to stop them discolouring.
2 Slice the banana and marinate in the lemon juice with the apple.
3 Halve the grapes and remove the seeds.
4 Slice the celery thinly to form crescents.
5 Mix the apples, bananas (and the lemon juice), grapes and celery together with the mayonnaise and season to taste.

Service

Dress a salad bowl or individual crescents with the lettuce, then neatly spoon the salad into the middle and sprinkle the pistachio nuts over the top.

Uses

Buffets or single hors-d'oeuvres.

Salade d'Albignac
CHICKEN AND CELERIAC SALAD

Portions: 4

Quantity		Ingredients	
200g	8oz	white of chicken	cooked
100g	4oz	celeriac	peeled
10g	½oz	garnishing paste	sliced
250ml	½ pint	mayonnaise	
		salt and pepper	
Garnish			
50g	2oz	scampi tails	poached
	1 bunch	watercress	washed and dried
	2	eggs	hard-boiled and cut into wedges

Method

1 Cut the chicken into fine julienne, reserving a little and slicing it.
2 Cut the celeriac into fine julienne.
3 Cut the garnishing paste into fine julienne.
4 Mix the chicken, celeriac and garnishing paste together and with the mayonnaise.
5 Season to taste.

Service

Serve loosely domed in a white SUR LE PLAT DISH garnished with the reserved slices of chicken, the scampi tails, the watercress and the egg wedges.

Uses

Buffets or as required, table d'hôte hors-d'oeuvres or hors-d'oeuvre varié.

Salade de Boeuf

BEEF SALAD

Portions: 4

Quantity		Ingredients	Preparation
100g	4oz	cooked ox tongue	sliced
100g	4oz	cooked beef	sliced
50g	2oz	onion	shredded
	1	red pepper	de-seeded and quartered
	1	green pepper	de-seeded and quartered
		salt and pepper	
¼ x	recipe	French Mustard Dressing (see page 15)	
5g	¼oz	garnishing paste	cut into julienne
50g	½oz	gherkin	cut into julienne

Method

1 Carefully cut the ox tongue and beef into a julienne.
2 Mix the onion with the meats.
3 Finely julienne the peppers and mix with the meat.
4 Season the mixture and moisten with the French Mustard Dressing.

Service

Spoon the salad neatly into a white SUR LE PLAT DISH, doming it slightly. Decorate with the garnishing paste and gherkin, sprinkling them over the salad.

Uses

Buffets, table d'hôte hors-d'oeuvres or hors-d'oeuvre varié.

Variation

As above but use 200g (8oz) cooked shin of beef instead of the ox tongue and beef and omit the garnishing paste for Salade Jarret de Boeuf.

Salade de Deux Pommes

TWO APPLE SALAD

Portions: 4

Quantity		Ingredients	Preparation
200g	8oz	potatoes	
200g	8oz	dessert apples	peeled and cored
250ml	½ pint	mayonnaise	
		salt and pepper	
	1	lettuce	washed and dried

Method

1 Cook the potatoes in their jackets, refresh, peel off the skin and cut the potato into small dice.
2 Cut the apples into small dice.
3 Mix the potatoes and apples together.
4 Mix the mayonnaise in with them.
5 Season to taste.

Service

Serve the salad on a bed of the lettuce, arranged in a salad bowl.

Uses

Buffets or as required.

Salade de Pommes de Terre

POTATO SALAD

Portions: 4

Quantity		Ingredients	Preparation
400g	1lb	potatoes	skins washed and scrubbed
25g	1oz	onions *or* chives	finely chopped
125ml	¼ pint	vinaigrette	
		salt and pepper	
250ml	½ pint	mayonnaise	
Garnish			
5g	¼oz	parsley	finely chopped

Method

1 Cook the potatoes in their jackets, then peel off the skins and cut the potato into dice.
2 Marinate the potatoes in the vinaigrette with the onions or chives until they are cold (about 30 minutes).
3 Drain the potatoes, season and mix in the mayonnaise.

Service

Spoon the salad neatly into a salad bowl and garnish by sprinkling the parsley over the top.

Uses

Buffets or as required.

Salade de Riz
RICE SALAD

Portions: 4

Quantity		Ingredients	Preparation
150g	6oz	rice	cooked and refreshed
50g	2oz	tomatoes	made into a CONCASSER
	¼	red pepper	finely diced
	¼	green pepper	finely diced
25g	1oz	sweetcorn	cooked and refreshed
25g	1oz	peas	cooked and refreshed
	¼	cucumber	finely diced
125ml	¼ pint	vinaigrette	
		salt and pepper	

Method

1 Mix all the ingredients together well.
2 Leave to marinate for 15–20 minutes before serving.

Service

Spoon the salad neatly into the serving dish.

Uses

Buffet or as required.

Salade de Viande
MEAT SALAD

Portions: 4

Quantity		Ingredients	Preparation
75g	3oz	ham	sliced
75g	3oz	beef	sliced
75g	3oz	ox tongue	sliced
100g	4oz	tomatoes	made into a CONCASSER
100g	4oz	French beans	cut into lozenges and cooked
10g	½oz	onions *or* chives	finely chopped
50g	2oz	gherkins	cut into julienne
5g	¼oz	parsley	finely chopped
125ml	¼ pint	vinaigrette	
Garnish			
	1	lettuce	washed and dried
	½	tomato	cut into wedges
	4	gherkins	sliced to form fans

Method

1 Cut the meat into fine julienne.
2 Mix all the ingredients together with the vinaigrette.
3 Season to taste.

Uses

Buffets or table d'hôte hors-d'oeuvres or hors-d'oeuvre varié.

Service

Arrange a bed of lettuce in the bottom of a RAVIER dish and spoon the salad neatly into the middle, doming it slightly. Garnish with the tomato wedges and gherkin fans.

Salade Eve

APPLE, PINEAPPLE AND BANANA SALAD

Portions: 4

Quantity		Ingredients	Preparation
	4	medium red dessert apples	cleaned
125ml	5fl oz	double cream	
		oil	
	2	medium green dessert apples	peeled and diced
	½	lemon	juiced
100g	4oz	pineapple	peeled, cored and diced
	2	bananas	peeled and diced
	1	lettuce	washed and dried

Method

1 Cut a thin slice from the bottom of each apple so it will not rock.
2 Remove the top and save.
3 Remove the flesh from inside with a PARISIENNE CUTTER to make a shell.
4 Brush the shells and lids very lightly with oil so that they shine attractively.
5 Whip the cream until it just begins to peak, then fold in the lemon juice.
6 Gently mix in the diced fruit.

Service

Fill the apple shells with the fruit and cream mixture. Replace the lids and serve on a bed of lettuce.

Uses

À la carte salad and table d'hôte hors-d'oeuvres.

Salade Florida/
Salade à l'Orange

ORANGE SALAD

Portions: 4

Quantity	Ingredients	Preparation
8	oranges	
1	lettuce heart	washed and dried

Method

1 Peel just the zest from the oranges and cut it into fine julienne.
2 Blanch and refresh the zest.
3 Peel the pith from the oranges and separate them into segments. Squeeze the juice from the segments of one orange.

Service

Place the lettuce heart leaves on a salad crescent, then arrange the orange segments neatly on top. Sprinkle the zest over top. NAPPER the salad with a little of the orange juice.

Uses

A delicious accompaniment to roast duckling.

Salade Francillon

MUSSEL AND POTATO SALAD

Portions: 4

Quantity		Ingredients	Preparation
200g	8oz	mussels	cooked and beards removed
125ml	¼ pint	vinaigrette	
200g	8oz	potatoes	
250ml	½ pint	white wine	
50g	2oz	shallots	finely chopped and blanched
		salt and pepper	
Garnish			
	1	lettuce	washed and dried
5g	¼oz	parsley	finely chopped
10g	½oz	garnishing paste	cut into julienne

Method

1 Marinate the mussels in the vinaigrette for 30 minutes.
2 Cook the potatoes in their jackets, then peel them, dice the flesh and marinate in the white wine for 30 minutes.
3 Mix all the ingredients (except the garnish ingredients) together and season to taste.

Uses

Buffets or table d'hôte hors-d'oeuvres or hors-d'oeuvre varié.

Service

Serve the salad in a white SUR LE PLAT DISH on a bed of the lettuce. Sprinkle the parsley and julienne of garnishing paste over the top and chill before serving.

Salade Italienne
ITALIAN SALAD

Portions: 4

Quantity		Ingredients	Preparation
150g	6oz	carrots	peeled and cut into julienne, saving a small piece
150g	6oz	turnips	peeled and cut into julienne, saving a small piece
150g	6oz	swede	peeled and cut into julienne, saving a small piece
125ml	¼ pint	vinaigrette	
50g	2oz	ham	sliced
50g	2oz	ox tongue	sliced
50g	2oz	salami	sliced
10g	½oz	anchovy fillets	cut into strips
25g	1oz	gherkins	cut into julienne, reserving 1
		salt and pepper	

Method

1 Cook the vegetable julienne separately until *al dente* (just cooked, not soft).
2 Drain and refresh in the vinaigrette.
3 Cut the meats into julienne.
4 Drain the vegetables and mix them with the meats, anchovy strips and gherkin.
5 Season to taste.
6 Cook and refresh the reserved small pieces of carrot, turnip and swede.
7 Cut each into a cylinder using a column cutter and slice thinly.
8 Slice the reserved gherkin into slices the same size as the others.

Service

Serve the salad on a white SUR LE PLAT DISH and garnish with the sliced vegetables, arranging them in strips to represent the Italian flag.

Uses

Buffets or table d'hôte hors-d'oeuvres or hors-d'oeuvre varié.

Variation

As above but replace the meats with 50g (2oz) each of ham, garlic sausage, cervelat and salami, the anchovy fillets with 50g (2oz) dill pickle and omit the gherkins and the reserving of vegetables for garnishing, using instead simply 4 gherkins, sliced to form fans for Salade de Viande.

Salade Japonaise

JAPANESE SALAD

Portions: 4

Quantity		Ingredients	Preparation
400g	1lb	tomatoes	made into a CONCASSER
10g	½oz	sugar	
		salt and pepper	
	1	lemon	juiced
200g	8oz	pineapple	skinned and cored
	1	orange	juiced
Garnish			
	1	lettuce	washed and dried
125ml	5fl oz	whipping cream	lightly whipped
	½	lemon	juiced

Method

1 To the tomato CONCASSER add the sugar, salt, pepper and half the lemon juice and marinate for 30 minutes.
2 Marinate the pineapple in the remaining lemon juice and the orange juice for 30 minutes.

Service

Arrange the lettuce leaves to form a border around the edge of a salad bowl. Then arrange the pineapple in a ring inside the lettuce ring. Spoon the tomato CONCASSER into the middle. Mix the cream and lemon juice together and serve in a sauce-boat to accompany the salad.

Uses

Buffets.

Salade Mercedes

MARINATED VEGETABLE AND EGG SALAD

Portions: 4

Quantity		Ingredients	Preparation
100g	4oz	celery	
100g	4oz	beetroot	cooked
	2	endives	trimmed and washed
100g	4oz	tomatoes	blanched and skinned
250ml	½ pint	vinaigrette	
Garnish			
	1	lettuce	washed and dried
	1	egg	hard-boiled
5g	¼oz	parsley	finely chopped
10g	½oz	garnishing paste	cut into julienne

Method

1 Cut the vegetables into fine julienne and put into a bowl.
2 Pour the vinaigrette over the vegetables and marinate for 30 minutes.
3 Remove the shell from the hard-boiled egg, separate the white and yolk and sieve.

Service

Arrange a bed of lettuce on a salad crescent. Place BOUQUETS of the vegetable julienne on the dish and, at either end, the sieved egg yolk and white. Decorate with the parsley and garnishing paste and chill before serving.

Uses

À la carte salad.

Salade Mexicaine

MEXICAN SALAD

Portions: 4

Quantity		Ingredients	
200g	8oz	breast of chicken	poached
100g	4oz	celeriac	peeled
100g	4oz	red peppers	blanched, skinned, and de-seeded
5g	¼oz	saffron	
250ml	½ pint	vinaigrette	
50g	2oz	onions	finely chopped
	2	eggs	hard-boiled, refreshed and shelled
		salt and pepper	
5g	¼oz	chives	finely chopped
	1	endive	trimmed, washed and dried

Method

1 Cut the chicken into fine julienne.
2 Cut the celeriac into julienne and blanch.
3 Cut the red pepper into fine julienne.
4 Mix the saffron with the vinaigrette.
5 Marinate the chicken, celeriac, red pepper and onions in the vinaigrette for 30 minutes.
6 Season to taste.
7 Cut the eggs into quarters.

Service

Separate the leaves from the endive and arrange in a salad bowl or on each individual serving plate. Spoon the marinated salad into the middle and garnish with the eggs and chives.

Uses

Buffets or hors-d'oeuvres.

Salade Niçoise

FRENCH SALAD

Portions: 4

Quantity		Ingredients	Preparation
100g	4oz	potatoes	
125g	¼ pint	vinaigrette	
200g	8oz	french beans	cooked and cut into lozenges
50g	2oz	tomatoes	made into a CONCASSER
		salt and pepper	
Optional			
50g	2oz	onions	finely chopped
100g	4oz	tuna fish	drained and flaked
Garnish			
10g	½oz	anchovy fillets	cut into strips
10g	½oz	black olives	stoned and halved
50g	2oz	tomatoes	blanched, skinned and cut into wedges

Method

1 Cook the potatoes in their jackets, remove the skin and cut the potato into small dice.
2 Marinate the potatoes in the vinaigrette (reserving a tablespoon for later) for 30 minutes.
3 Just before serving mix in the French beans, tomato CONCASSER, onions and tuna fish, if using, and season to taste.

Service

Spoon the salad neatly into a SUR LE PLAT DISH, doming the mixture slightly. Decorate the top in the traditional way, placing the anchovy fillets in a trellis pattern, the olives in the diamonds and the wedges of tomato, brushed with the reserved vinaigrette, around the edge.

Uses

Buffets or table d'hôte hors-d'oeuvres.

Salade Normande

NORMANDY SALAD

Portions: 4

Quantity		Ingredients	Preparation
100g	4oz	beetroot	cooked and peeled
125ml	¼ pint	vinaigrette	
200g	8oz	dessert apples	peeled and cored
125ml	¼ pint	double cream	whipped until it forms peaks
	1	lemon	juiced
		salt and pepper	

Method

1 Cut the beetroot into short thickish julienne.
2 Marinate them in the vinaigrette for 30 minutes.
3 Cut the apples into short thickish julienne.
4 Gently mix the cream and lemon juice together.
5 Mix the cream with the apple and season to taste.
6 Drain the beetroot.

Service

Border a RAVIER dish neatly with the beetroot, then spoon the apple and cream mixture into the middle.

Uses

Buffets or as required.

Salade Poivron

PEPPER SALAD

Portions: 4

Quantity		Ingredients	Preparation
	1	red pepper	
	1	green pepper	
	1	yellow pepper	
	1	black pepper	
	1	orange pepper	
100g	4oz	onion	shredded
125ml	¼ pint	vinaigrette	

Method

1 Cut the peppers in half lengthways and remove the stalks and seeds.
2 Trim off the ribs from inside.
3 Cut the pepper halves into quarters.
4 Cut the quarters into fine julienne across their width.
5 Mix the pepper julienne and the onion together.
6 Moisten with the vinaigrette and mix it in well, ensuring that the different colours are evenly distributed.

Uses

Service

Spoon the salad neatly into a RAVIER or salad bowl.

Salade Russe

RUSSIAN SALAD

Portions: 4

Quantity		Ingredients	Preparation
200g	8oz	swede	scrubbed and peeled
200g	8oz	turnip	scrubbed and peeled
200g	8oz	carrots	scrubbed and peeled
50g	2oz	petits pois	
100g	4oz	French beans	topped and tailed
250ml	½ pint	vinaigrette	
250ml	½ pint	mayonnaise	
		salt and pepper	

Method

1 Cut the swede, turnip and carrots into even-sized, short, thickish julienne.
2 Cook each of the vegetables separately until they are *al dente* (just cooked, not soft).
3 Drain them and leave them in the vinaigrette until they have completely cooled.
4 Cook the petits pois and cool under running water until cold, then add to the vinaigrette.
5 Cook the beans, cool under running water until cold, then cut into lozenges.
6 Drain the marinade from the vegetables and mix them with the beans.
7 Mix all the vegetables together with the mayonnaise.
8 Season to taste.

Service

Spoon the salad neatly into a salad bowl or RAVIER as required.

Uses

Buffets or as required.

Salade Waldorf
WALDORF SALAD

Portions: 4

Quantity		Ingredients	Preparation
100g	4oz	celery	washed
200g	8oz	dessert apples	peeled and cored
	1	lemon	juiced
10g	½oz	walnut halves	
250ml	½ pint	mayonnaise	
		salt and pepper	
	1	lettuce	washed and dried

Method

1 Cut the celery and apple into short, thickish julienne.
2 Marinate the apples in the lemon juice while completing the recipe to prevent them discolouring.
3 Drain the apples and mix them with the celery and half of the walnuts.
4 Mix in the mayonnaise.
5 Season to taste and chill until required.

Service

Arrange the lettuce in the bottom of the serving dish, spoon the salad into the middle and garnish it with the reserved walnut halves.

Uses

Buffets or as required.

8
SIMPLE SALADS

Salade de Betterave

BEETROOT SALAD

Portions: 4

Quantity		Ingredients	Preparation
200g	8oz	beetroot	well washed
10g	½oz	onions *or* chives	finely chopped
125ml	¼ pint	vinaigrette	
Garnish			
5g	¼oz	parsley	finely chopped

Method

1 Place the beetroot in a saucepan full of cold water, cover with a lid and bring to boil.
2 Simmer until tender.
3 Leave to cool, then remove the skin.
4 Cut into short, thickish julienne.
5 Mix carefully with the onions or chives and vinaigrette.

Uses

Service

Neatly spoon the salad into a RAVIER dish and garnish by sprinkling the chopped parsley over the top.

Salade de Choux Cru

RAW WHITE CABBAGE SALAD

Portions: 4

Quantity		Ingredients
400g	1lb	white cabbage
125ml	¼ pint	vinaigrette

Method

1 Remove any damaged outer leaves from the cabbage.
2 Cut it into quarters and remove the stalk.
3 Shred finely.
4 Wash and dry.

Service

Spoon the shredded cabbage neatly into a serving dish. Serve the vinaigrette separately.

Uses

_____

_____

_____

Salade de Concombre

CUCUMBER SALAD

Portions: 4

Quantity		Ingredients	Preparation
	½	cucumber	peeled and thinly sliced
125ml	¼ pint	vinaigrette	
25g	1oz	onions	finely chopped
5g	¼oz	parsley	finely chopped

Method

1 Place the cucumber slices neatly down the centre of a RAVIER dish, slightly overlapping them. NAPPER with vinaigrette.
2 Chill until about to serve.

Service

Place a fine, neat line of onions down the middle of the cucumber, then place a fine line of parsley on the onions.

Uses

Variation

As above but use 200 (8oz) blanched, skinned and sliced tomatoes for Salade de Tomates.

Salade d'Haricots Verts

FRENCH GREEN BEAN SALAD

Portions: 4

Quantity		Ingredients	Preparation
200g	8oz	fine French beans	topped and tailed
125ml	¼ pint	vinaigrette	
		salt and pepper	

Method

1 Cook the French beans until *al dente* (just cooked, not soft) in boiling salted water.
2 Refresh under cold running water until cold.
3 Drain until they are dry.
4 Cut into even lozenges.

Service

Just before serving, mix the beans with the vinaigrette, season, then spoon into a RAVIER dish.

Salade Endive Frisée

CURLY CHICORY LETTUCE SALAD

Portions: 10

Quantity	Ingredients	Preparation
2	curly chicory lettuces	washed and dried

Method

1 Trim any damaged outer leaves, then separate the leaves from the stem.
2 Plunge into deep, salted water several times to wash them thoroughly.
3 Remove the leaves from the water and leave them to drain until they are dry.

Service

Place the leaves neatly in a salad bowl using the outer leaves for the outside of the bowl working to the centre.

Uses

Buffets or as an accompaniment to roast dishes.

Variations

As above but use 5 chicory *or* endive, cut them into 5 or 6 wedges and arrange in a star shape in a bowl for Salade Endive Belge.

As above, but use the same number of cos lettuces for Salade Laitne Romaine or round lettuces for plain Salade de Laitne.

As above but use 1 each of round lettuce, radicchio, chicory, oak leaf lettuce and lamb's lettuce, arranging them in such a way as to show the different colours off to best advantage for Salade de Laitne Colors.

Salade Française avec Vinaigrette

FRENCH MIXED SALAD WITH VINAIGRETTE

Portions: 10

Quantity		Ingredients	Preparation
	3	iceberg lettuces	washed, dried and shredded
200g	8oz	beetroot	cooked, skinned and cut as required
	4	eggs	hard-boiled and shelled, cut as required
250ml	½ pint	vinaigrette	
5g	¼oz	fresh tarragon	washed and finely chopped

Method

1 Add the finely chopped tarragon to the vinaigrette.

Service

Arrange the lettuce neatly in a salad bowl. Arrange the egg in a ring inside the outside edge of the lettuce and put the beetroot inside this ring. Mix the vinaigrette with the tarragon and serve the tarragon vinaigrette separately in a sauce-boat.

Uses

Buffets or as an accompaniment to roast dishes.

Salade Panachée Française

FRENCH MIXED SALAD

Portions: 10

Quantity		Ingredients	Preparation
	2 bunches	spring onions	trimmed and washed
	1 bunch	radishes	cleaned
	2	round lettuces	washed and dried
	1 bunch	watercress	washed, dried and trimmed
	2	endive	washed, dried and cut into 4–6 wedges
	1	cucumber	grooves cut along it with a CANELLE KNIFE and thinly sliced
200g	8oz	tomatoes	blanched, skinned and cut into wedges
	2	eggs	hard-boiled, shelled and cut into wedges
125ml	¼ pint	vinaigrette	

Method

1 Slice the white ends of the spring onions very finely along their length and place in iced water for about an hour until the slices have curled to make spring onion flowers.

2 Make radish flowers by removing the stalks and making cuts almost all the way through, as if cutting portions for a round cake, then place them in iced water for several hours until they open out.

Service

Place all the ingredients neatly into a salad bowl in the following order: place the outer leaves of the lettuce at the outside edge of the bowl and work towards the centre; place the watercress in the centre; border the outside edge of the bowl with the endive wedges and spring onion flowers; border the inside edge of the lettuce with the cucumber, overlapping the slices; place the tomato wedges and radish flowers neatly inside the cucumber; place the wedges of hard-boiled egg neatly inside this ring but outside the watercress. Dribble the vinaigrette evenly over the arranged salad.

Uses

Buffets or as an accompaniment to roast dishes.

Variation

As above but without the radishes, tomatoes and eggs for Salade Verte.

Salade Panachée

MIXED SALAD

Portions: 10

Quantity		Ingredients	
	2 bunches	spring onions	trimmed
	2	red peppers	de-seeded
	2	green peppers	de-seeded
	2	yellow peppers	de-seeded
	1	curly endive lettuce	washed and dried
	1	Chinese leaf lettuce	washed and dried
	1	radicchio	washed and dried
400g	1lb	tomatoes	blanched, skinned and cut into wedges
400g	1lb	red onions	shredded or cut into thin rings

Method

1 Cut the peppers into fine julienne and keep the colours separate.
2 Make the spring onions into flowers (see page 246).

Service

Arrange the different lettuce leaves attractively in a salad bowl, using the outer leaves for the outside of the bowl and working in to the centre. Border the outside of the bowl with the spring onion flowers and the inside edge of the lettuce with BOUQUETS of red, green and yellow julienne of pepper. Place the tomato wedges neatly inside the ring of peppers and the red onion in the middle.

Uses

Buffets.

Variations

As above but use 3 Chinese leaf lettuces instead of the different lettuces and omit the tomatoes for Salade en Saison.

As above but use 2 iceberg lettuces and 2 Chinese leaf lettuces, omit the radicchio, just 2 green peppers (omit the red and yellow ones) and 200g (8oz) fennel (stalk removed and cut into fine julienne) for the centre for Salade Verte.

9
WARM SALADS

Salad of Monkfish Tails Chinese Style

Portions: 4

Quantity		Ingredients	Preparation
250g	8oz	monkfish tails	skinned and cleaned
75ml	⅛ pint	soy sauce	
25g	1oz	sesame seeds	
100g	4oz	spring onions	washed and sliced
100g	4oz	beansprouts	washed
	1	lemon	juiced
	1	lime	juiced
		salt and pepper	
250g	8oz	salad leaves	
75ml	⅛ pint	sesame oil	

Method

1 Slice the monkfish tail and marinate in the soya sauce, lemon and lime juices for approximately 30 minutes.
2 Quickly saute the monkfish tails, beansprouts and the sliced spring onions in a little sesame seed oil; add the marinade and sesame seeds; season.

Service

Dress the salad leaves in a little of the sauce and place in the centre of the plate. Arrange the fish and vegetables in the centre of the leaves and serve. This salad must be served warm.

Warm Chicken Liver Salad

Portions: 4

Quantity		Ingredients	Preparation
250g	8oz	chicken livers	marinated
50g	2oz	croûtons	
	1 clove	garlic	crushed
75ml	⅛ pint	olive oil	
75ml	⅛ pint	Madeira	
250g	8oz	salad leaves	washed
		salt and pepper	

Method

1 Marinate the chicken livers in the Madeira for approximately 1 hour.
2 Fry the croûtons in a little olive oil; keep warm.
3 Sauté the livers quickly in the hot olive oil, seasoning with salt, pepper and garlic. The livers must be served pink.
4 Remove from the pan and keep with the croûtons, deglaze the pan with the Madeira; boil and keep.

Service

Arrange the salad leaves in the centre of the plate. Place the livers and the croûtons in the centre of the leaves, pour over a little of the marinade and serve. This salad must be served warm.

Uses

Warm Goose Liver Salad with a Raspberry Vinaigrette

Portions: 4

Quantity		Ingredients	Preparation
250g	8oz	*foie gras*	sliced thinly
125ml	¼ pint	raspberry vinegar	
125ml	¼ pint	olive oil *or* walnut oil	
100g	4oz	tomato CONCASSER	
250g	8oz	salad leaves	
25g	1oz	chervil	
		salt and pepper	

Method

1 Prepare a vinaigrette with the raspberry vinegar and the oil; season to taste.
2 Very quickly sauté the *foie gras* without adding any oil; season with salt and pepper; keep warm.

Service

Dress the salad leaves in a little of the vinaigrette, and arrange in the centre of the plate. Place 4 neat piles of tomato CONCASSER on each plate. Arrange the sliced *foie gras* on top of the leaves, sprinkle with the vinaigrette and garnish with the fresh chervil leaves and serve. This salad must be served warm.

Warm Melon and Honey Salad

Portions: 4

Quantity		Ingredients	Preparation
	1	Ogen melon	
100g	4oz	clear honey	
25g	1oz	sesame seeds	
50g	2oz	fresh mint	washed
100g	4oz	fresh strawberries	

Method

1 Cut the melon into quarters and skin.
2 Cut each slice into a fan.
3 Place a slice onto a plate and grill for 30 seconds; remove and coat with warm honey; place back under the grill.
4 Remove; sprinkle with the sesame seeds and grill until the seeds are golden brown.

Service

Place on a warm plate and decorate with the fresh strawberries and the sprigs of fresh mint. Serve warm.

Warm Mushroom Salad

Portions: 4

Quantity		Ingredients	Preparation
300g	12oz	mushrooms (cepes, morels, oyster, chanterelles, button) – a selection	sliced
50g	2oz	unsalted butter salt and pepper	
50g	2oz	parsley	chopped
250g	8oz	salad leaves	washed
125ml	¼ pint	dijon vinaigrette	

Method

1 Wash the salad leaves.
2 Wash the mushrooms.
3 Sauté the mushrooms quickly in the unsalted butter; season; add chopped parsley and mix well together.

Service

Dress the salad leaves with a little of the Dijon vinaigrette and place in the centre of the plate. Spoon on the mushrooms; sprinkle with a little of the vinaigrette, and serve. This salad must be served warm.

Warm Salad of Quails' Eggs and Lardons

Portions: 4

Quantity		Ingredients	Preparation
	12	quails' eggs	
250g	8oz	bacon lardons	
250g	8oz	salad leaves	washed
75ml	⅛ pint	walnut oil	
75ml	⅛ pint	white wine vinegar	
		salt and pepper	
25g	1oz	fresh tarragon	

Method

1 Poach the quails' eggs for approximately 2 minutes; refresh and keep in iced water until service.
2 Sauté the lardons in a little of the oil; keep warm.
3 Whisk the oil and vinegar together and season.
4 Plunge the quails' eggs into the poaching liquid for 30 seconds, drain.

Service

Dress the salad leaves in the vinaigrette and arrange in the centre of the plate. Place the quails' eggs and lardons onto the leaves; pour over a little of the vinaigrette; and garnish with a little fresh tarragon. This salad must be served warm.

Warm Salad of Scallops and Lobster with a Hazelnut Vinaigrette

Portions: 4

Quantity		Ingredients	Preparation
250g	8oz	scallops	sliced
250g	8oz	lobster tail	sliced
	1	lemon	juiced
25g	1oz	dill	chopped
25g	1oz	chervil	chopped
25g	1oz	parsley	chopped
25g	1oz	coriander	chopped
250g	8oz	salad leaves	washed
150ml	¼ pint	hazelnut oil	
150ml	¼ pint	white wine vinegar	
		salt and pepper	

Method

1 Marinate the lobster tails and the scallops in the lemon juice and all the herbs for approximately 1 hour.

2 Quickly sauté the fish in a little of the hazelnut oil, season.

3 Whisk the oil, vinegar and the marinade together, season.

Service

Dress the salad leaves in the
vinaigrette and place in the centre of
the plate. Arrange the lobster and
the scallops in the centre of the
leaves and pour over a little of the
vinaigrette. This salad must be
served warm.

Uses

Warm Scallop Salad

Portions: 4

Quantity		Ingredients	Preparation
250g	8oz	fresh scallops	sliced
	1	lemon	juiced
	1	lime	juiced
	2	pink grapefruit	segmented
25g	1oz	fresh dill	
250g	8oz	fresh salad leaves	washed
		salt and pepper	
75ml	⅛ pint	French dressing	

Method

1 Slice the scallops, season with salt and pepper and marinate in the fruit juices, for 30 minutes.
2 Drain and quickly sauté in a little olive oil, for approximately 1 minute, and add the fruit juices.
3 Remove the scallops and drain on a little kitchen paper. Boil the juice and use to dress the scallops for service.
4 Wash the salad leaves (any type may be used, e.g. curly endive, batavia, lambs leaf, raddicchio).

Service

Dress the salad leaves in a little French dressing; season; and place in the centre of the plate. Arrange the scallops and pink grapefruit segments on top of the salad leaves; pour over the warm fruit juices; and garnish with sprigs of fresh dill. This salad must be served warm.

Uses

10
PÂTÉS AND TERRINES

Appareil de Pâtés/Terrines

BASIC PÂTÉ

Portions: 8–10

Quantity		Ingredients	Preparation
1kg	2lb	liver	trimmed, removing the gall
400g	1lb	lean meat	trimmed, sinew removed and diced
400g	1lb	fat/bacon	trimmed and diced
Seasoning			
5g	¼oz	Sel d'Épice (see page 5)	
5g	¼oz	Épice de Charcutière (see page 3)	
		salt and pepper	
Marinade			
125ml	¼ pint	brandy	
125 or	¼ or	dry sherry *or* port	
250ml	½ pint	*or* red wine	
Lining for moulds			
200g	½lb	back fat *or* streaky bacon *or* caul fat	thinly sliced *or* trimmed and hammered out until thin *or* soaked in salt water and trimmed
500ml	1 pint	aspic (see page 4)	

Method

1 Day 1, place the prepared meats in a container, add the seasoning and marinade, cover and marinate for 24 hours, turning as required.

2 Day 2, mince the meats as required, line and fill moulds, cover with paper lids and the lid.

3 Day 3, cook the pâtés in bain-maries as required, test, place a 1kg (2lb) weight on top and leave to cool.

Service

Day 4, clean the surface of the pâtés pour in a layer of aspic and cool until it has set. Day 5, serve the pâtés as a terrine to be shared by several diners or slice and glaze individual portions. Decorate as required.

Uses

Single hors-d'oeuvres.

Variations

As above using 1kg (2lb) pigs' livers, 400g (1lb) lean pork and 400g(1lb) fat or bacon, marinating with 250ml (½pint) red wine and lining the moulds with 200g (½lb) back fat and mincing the meats coarsely in step 2 for Pâté de Campagne.

As above using 1kg (2lb) chicken livers, 400g (1lb) lean chicken and 400g (1lb) fat or bacon, adding 100g (4oz) finely grated Stilton and the same amount of blanched, skinned and chopped walnuts to the meats on day 2 and mincing them together if desired, lining the moulds with 200g (½lb) back fat for Pâté Foie de Volaille.

As above using 1kg (2lb) chicken and game livers, 400g (1lb) lean game and 400g (1lb) bacon, marinating with 500ml (½ pint) red wine or 125ml (¼ pint) port and lining the moulds with 200g (½lb) streaky bacon, hammered until it is thin, and mincing the meats coarsely in step 2 for Terrine de Gibier.

As above using 1kg (2lb) chicken livers, 400g (1lb) lean chicken and 400g (1lb) fat or bacon, adding 50g (2oz) roughly chopped green peppercorns on day 2 and mincing them together and lining the moulds with 200g (½lb) back fat for Terrine de Volaille au Poivre Vert.

As above using 400g (1lb) pigs' livers, 400g (1lb) chicken livers, 400g (1lb) lean pork and 400g (1lb) fat or bacon and lining the moulds with 200g (½lb) back fat for Terrine pur Porc.

La Marinade Cru au Vin Blanc

WHITE WINE MARINADE

Portions: 10

Quantity		Ingredients	Preparation
5g	¼oz	Sel d'Épice (see page 5)	
100g	4oz	onions	peeled and sliced
50g	2oz	carrots	peeled and sliced
25g	1 oz	celery	washed and sliced
25g	1 oz	leek	washed and sliced
10g	½oz	parsley stalks	washed
	10	peppercorns	
	1	clove	
	2 sprigs	thyme	
500ml	1 pint	white wine	
125ml	¼ pint	oil	

Method

1 Rub the meat with the Sel d'Épice and put it into a stainless steel or plastic container.
2 Sprinkle vegetables, herbs and spices over the meat.
3 Moisten with the liquids.
4 Cover with plastic lid or cling film.
5 Store in a fridge and turn twice daily for about 5–7 days before cooking the meat.

Uses

To improve the flavour of veal and poultry.

La Marinade Cru au Vin Rouge Pour Gibier

RED WINE MARINADE FOR GAME

Portions: 10

Quantity		Ingredients	Preparation
100g	4oz	onions	sliced
50g	2oz	carrots	peeled and sliced
25g	1oz	celery	washed and chopped
25g	1oz	leek	washed and chopped
10g	½oz	parsley stalks	washed
500ml	1 pint	red wine	
125ml	¼ pint	oil	
	10	peppercorns	
	1	clove	
	2 sprigs	thyme	
	8	coriander seeds	
	8	juniper berries	
5g	¼oz	Sel d'Épice (see page 5)	
Optional			
	1 clove	garlic	crushed

Method

1 Mix all the vegetables, liquids and spices together, including the garlic, if using, except the Sel d'Épice.
2 Rub the game to be marinated with the Sel d'Épice.
3 Place the meat in the marinade, cover and refrigerate.
4 Turn the meat twice daily for about 1–2 weeks, depending on the size of the joints (marinate larger joints longer than smaller ones).

Uses

Usually used for venison and hare to improve the flavour.

Parfait de Foies de Volaille

CHICKEN PARFAIT WITH CHICKEN LIVER

Portions: 8–10

Quantity		Ingredients	Preparation
275g	11oz	lean chicken	
		Sel d'Épice (see page 5)	
		salt and white pepper	
	1 pinch	ground ginger	
	1 pinch	cardamom pods	grind
	1	egg white	
75g	3oz	Panada (see page 7)	
550ml	12fl oz	whipping cream	whipped
125ml	5oz	chicken livers	
	1tbsp	oil	
		butter for greasing	
500ml	1 pint	Maderia aspic (see page 4)	
	3tbsp	parsley	finely chopped

Method

1 Cut the chicken into strips, sprinkle with the seasoning and chill for 2–3 hours.

2 Mince it twice using the fine plate on a mincer.

3 Over ice, beat in the egg white and panada.

4 Push the mixture through a fine sieve.

5 Beat in the cream, a spoonful at a time.

6 Trim the chicken livers, cut them into small pieces, fry them quickly in the oil, drain and fold into the chicken and cream mixture.

7 Line a buttered mould with roasting film, add the chicken and cream mixture and smooth the top. Fold film over the mixture and cover.

8 Cook it in a bain-marie for about 40 minutes.
9 When it has cooled, turn it out onto a serving plate and carefully peel off the film.
10 Cover it with some of the Maderia aspic, sprinkle the parsley over the top and cover again with aspic. Pour any remaining aspic in a thin layer on a flat dish and, when it has set, cut it into diamonds.

Service

Slice the Parfait into 50–75g (2–3oz) portions, place each on a plate and garnish with the Maderia aspic diamonds.

Uses

_____

_____

_____

Variations

As above but fry 125g (5oz) finely chopped mushrooms and add them to the chicken and cream mixture with the chicken livers for Parfait de Foies de Volaille aux Champignons.

Derivatives

_____

_____

_____

Terrine Covent Garden

VEGETABLE TERRINE

Portions: 15

Quantity		Ingredients	Preparation
250g	10oz	artichoke bottoms (tinned)	drained
50g	2oz	mushrooms	washed and dried
100g	4oz	mange-tout	topped and tailed
200g	8oz	French green beans	topped and tailed
1kg	2lb	broccoli	trimmed and cut into florets
400g	1lb	carrots	scrubbed
400g	1lb	courgettes	sliced in half and slightly hollowed out
100g	4oz	butter	
Farce de Volaille			
400g	1lb	chicken	DE-NERVED
500ml	1 pint	double cream	
		salt and pepper	
Sauce			
500ml	1 pint	aspic (see page 4)	
1 x	recipe	Terrine Covent Garden Sauce (see page 37)	

Method

1 Blanch and refresh the vegetables.
2 See Farce de Poisson, page 173, for method for Farce de Volaille.
3 Fill a terrine in the following way – vegetables, Farce, vegetables until full, then fill the hollowed out courgettes with the remaining Farce and put them in the centre of the terrine.
4 Cover it and poach for 35–45 minutes.
5 Pour the aspic over the top and leave to cool until it has set.

Service

Cut the Terrine into 1.5-cm (½-inch) thick slices, lay them in the centre of each serving plate and pour a CORDON of the sauce around them.

Uses

_____

_____

_____

Variations

Cook other vegetables *al dente* (just cooked, not soft) and set with aspic in layers, using any suitable seasonal types of vegetables available.

Derivatives

_____

_____

_____

Terrine de Lapereau du Chef
RABBIT TERRINE

Portions: 10–12

Quantity		Ingredients	Preparation
1½-kg	3-lb	rabbit	
250g	10oz	lean pork	diced
250g	10oz	pork fat	diced
	1	shallot	finely chopped
	1 clove	garlic	crushed
	1tsp	thyme	
125ml	5fl oz	red wine	
	2tbsp	orange juice	
	1tsp	orange zest	grated
		salt and pepper	
	1tbsp	oil	
	1	bouquet garni	
	1	carrot	sliced
	1	onion	quartered
	2	eggs	
	2tbsp	pistachio nuts	
	1	caul fat *or* back fat	thinly sliced
	2	bay leaves	
Sauce			
	1 bunch	parsley	
125ml	5fl oz	double cream	
125ml	5fl oz	mayonnaise	
Garnish			
	1	radicchio	

Method

1 Remove the meat from the rabbit, DE-NERVE, cut the fillets into fine strips and dice any remaining meat.

2 Place the fillet strips in a shallow dish at one end. Place the diced rabbit, pork, pork fat, shallot, garlic, thyme, wine, orange juice and zest, salt and black pepper at the other end.

3 Mix well and leave to marinate for 24 hours, turning the meats in the marinade once or twice.

4 Chop up the rabbit carcass, heat the oil in a roasting pan and brown the bones.

5 Add 750ml (1½ pints) of water, the bouquet garni, carrot and onion, bring to the boil, then simmer gently for 2 hours.

6 Strain the stock, return it to a clean pan and cook until it has reduced to 250ml (½ pint). Leave it to cool.

7 Remove the fillets from the marinade and set them to one side.

8 Finely chop the remaining meat, add the marinade, eggs and 175ml (7fl oz) of the reduced rabbit stock.

9 Mix well, then add the pistachio nuts.

10 Line a 1-litre (2-pint) terrine with the caul fat *or* pork back fat.

11 Spread a third of the meat mixture evenly in the bottom of the terrine, lay half the fillets on top, spread another third of the meat mixture on top, add the remaining fillets and, finally, the remaining meat mixture.

12 Press down well.

13 Cover the top with the slices of fat, place the bay leaves on top and cover with the lid.

14 Cook the terrine in a bain-marie for 1¼–1½ hours.

15 When cooked, place a 1kg (2lb) weight on top and leave until it has cooled and set.

16 To make the sauce, liquidise the parsley and remaining stock in a food processor or blender until smooth, then briefly blend in the cream and mayonnaise, season to taste, pass through a sieve to remove any remaining lumps and chill until needed for serving.

Service

NAPPER each serving plate with the sauce, arrange a bed of radicchio leaves on top, but in such a way that you can see the sauce round the edge, and finish with a slice of the rabbit terrine.

Uses

_____

_____

_____

Variations

Serve slices of the terrine with sauce-boats of sauce and salad bowls of radicchio.

Derivatives

_____

_____

Terrine de Lièvre au Porto

HARE TERRINE

Portions: 10–12

Quantity		Ingredients	Preparation
1kg	2lb	hare and liver	
100g	4oz	bacon	
125ml	5fl oz	brandy	
		salt and pepper	
	4	bay leaves	
	2	chicken livers	
100g	4oz	pork	
	2	shallots	finely chopped
	1 clove	garlic	crushed
	2	eggs	beaten
	1 sprig	thyme	leaves picked from stems, stems discarded

Garnish

500ml	1 pint	aspic (see page 4)	
25g	1oz	powdered gelatine	
375ml	¾ pint	consommé	
125ml	¼ pint	port	
	3	bay leaves	
	1tbsp	juniper berries	

Method

1 Cut the hare into thin strips and the bacon into large dice.
2 Marinate the meats in the brandy, salt, pepper and bay leaves for about 8 hours.
3 Chop the chicken livers and pork finely.

4 Gently fry the shallots, garlic and livers, then add them to the pork and add the marinated hare and bacon and strain the marinade over all these ingredients.

5 Add the beaten eggs and the leaves from the thyme and mix well together.
6 Spoon the mixture into a litre (2-pint) terrine, cover and bake at 300°F/150°C (Gas Mark 2) for 1½ hours.
7 Leave to cool.
8 Mix the aspic with the gelatine, consommé and port.
9 Decorate the terrine with the bay leaves and juniper berries and pour the aspic over the top.

Service

Serve either in the terrine with a bowl of salad *or* cut slices, decorate and glaze them and serve them on a plate with a salad garnish.

Uses

_____

_____

_____

Variations

_____

_____

_____

Derivatives

_____

_____

_____

Pâté de Jambon

HAM PÂTÉ

Portions: 8–10

Quantity		Ingredients	Preparation
2kg	4lb	lean cooked ham	
750ml	1½ pint	cold bechamel sauce	
		salt and pepper	
	1tsp	paprika	
500ml	½ pint	double cream	lightly whipped
200g	8oz	unsalted butter	melted
Garnish			
25g	1oz	fresh dill	washed and dried

Method

1 Trim any excess fat off the ham and cut the remaining lean meat into small dice.
2 Mince the diced ham twice using the fine plate in a mincer.
3 Mix the minced ham with the cold bechamel sauce.
4 Push this mixture through a fine wire sieve or blend in a food processor or blender.
5 Season to taste and add the paprika, mixing them in well.
6 Fold in the lightly whipped cream.
7 Fill a terrine or soufflé dish or individual ramekins with the mixture and smooth the top level.
8 Cover the top with a thin layer of the melted butter to seal it.
9 Put the pâté(s) in the refrigerator and chill until set.

Service

Decorate the top of the pâté(s) with crowns of dill and serve as required. Serve a suitable salad separately.

Uses

Table d'hôte hors-d'oeuvres.

Glossary of terms

Bouquet garnishes arranged in neat piles around foods.

Brunoise cut into fine dice.

Canelle knife grooved knife for cutting grooves into the skins of vegetables or fruit that are then sliced, giving the slices frilly edges, making them excellent for garnishing and decorating purposes.

Chiffonade a French term used to describe the process of cutting lettuce into fine strips or shredding it to sue as a garnish or bed for hors-d'oeuvres.

Chinois fine conical sieve.

Cisler to make fine cuts into whole round fish just where the fish is thickest (not near the tail).

Concasser a French word used to mean any food roughly or finely chopped, but in this book used specifically to refer to tomatoes that have been blanched, refreshed, skinned, de-seeded and coarsely or finely chopped according to use.

Cook out when a thickening mixture of water and starch is added to a sauce and it is heated and stirred until it thickens.

Cordon of sauce, poured onto plate in a thin line, usually round an individual food item.

Darnes of fish these are thick slices cut vertically down through the spine of round fish.

De-nerve this is done to rabbit and chicken by running a sharp knife alone the nerve, keeping knife and meat flat, and lifting it out.

Dish paper plain oval sheets of paper available in various sizes to fit FLATS.

Flat silver oval or round salver.

Mirror a FLAT flood a silver salver evenly with aspic and leave it to set.

Napper to coat.

Parisienne cutter tool with deep, round blade that is used to cut perfect balls from fruits, especially melons, and, occasionally, vegetables. It is available in a variety of sizes to suit the particular purpose.

Parisienne goblet wine glass.

Pluce just the heads of sprigs of parsley.

Ravier crescent-shaped shallow dish in which salad is served.

Salpicon to cut a mixture of ingredients into dice and bind them together with a sauce.

Set the claws of crayfish pin the main claws back so that they look as if they are rearing up for decorative purposes.

Silver cascade silver bowl on pedestal with rim over which prawns are laid.

Supremes of fish or chicken are thick slices cut on the slant from fillets of round fish or chicken.

Sur le plat dish round, shallow serving dish.

Tomato roses peel small tomatoes, taking some of the flesh as you go and making each edge of the strip gently uneven, then, with the flesh side outwards, wind the skin round and round to form a rosebud shape.

Turn mushrooms – to cut decorative sweeping curves into the caps from the centre down to the edges.

Van Dyke decorative cutting of spherical fruits and vegetables, such as lemons, melons, oranges and tomatoes, where a knife is inserted into the fruit or vegetable around its equator at alternate angles and then the two halves are pulled apart – each half then having a decorative zig zag edge.

Index